The Glass Air
Selected Poems

BOOKS BY P.K. PAGE

POETRY

As Ten as Twenty
The Metal and the Flower
Cry Ararat!
Poems Selected and New
Evening Dance of the Grey Flies
To Say the Least: Canadian Poets from A to Z (Editor)

FICTION

The Sun and the Moon and Other Fictions

P. K. PAGE
The Glass Air
Selected Poems

Toronto Oxford New York
OXFORD UNIVERSITY PRESS
1985

For Arthur

Many of the poems in this book have been selected from
*As Ten as Twenty, The Metal and the Flower, Cry Ararat!:
Poems New and Selected, Poems Selected and New* and
Evening Dance of the Grey Flies—all of which, with the
exception of the last, are out of print. The new poems
first appeared in *The Canadian Forum, Canadian Literature, The Malahat Review* and *Poetry Australia*. The
two essays are reprinted from *Canadian Literature,* and
art is reproduced by courtesy of the University of
Victoria, Joan Fraser, Mrs Philip Holmes, Dr Bernard
Naylor, M.A. Irwin, and W.A. Irwin.

Thanks are overdue to Margaret Atwood for editing *Poems
Selected and New,* to Constance Rooke and Rosemary
Sullivan for their informed and friendly reading of my work
and to Richard Teleky, two times editor, who makes it all
seem easy.

Canadian Cataloguing in Publication Data

Page, P.K. (Patricia Kathleen)
   The glass air : poems selected and new

ISBN 0-19-540506-4

I. Title.

PS8531.A43G57 1985   C811'.54   C85-099413-6
PR9199.3.P33G57 1985

Cover photograph: Paul Orenstein
© P.K. Page 1985
ISBN 0-19-540506-4
1 2 3 4 - 8 7 6 5
Printed in Canada by
Webcom Limited

Contents

DRAWING

ESSAYS

PERSONAL LANDSCAPE

Where the bog ends, there, where the ground lips, lovely
is love, not lonely.
                        Land is
love, round with it, where the hand is;
wide with love, cleared scrubland, grain
on a coin.
Oh, the wheat-field, the rock-bound rubble;
the untouched hills
                        as a thigh smooth;
the meadow.
Not only the poor soil lovely, the outworn prairie,
but the green upspringing,
the lark-land,
the promontory.

A lung-born land, this,
a breath spilling,
scanned by the valvular heart's
field glasses.

AS TEN AS TWENTY

For we can live now, love:
a million in us breathe,
moving as we move
and qualifying death

in lands our own and theirs
with simple hands as these
a walk as like as hers
and words as like as his.

They in us free our love
make archways of our mouths,
tear off the patent gloves
and atrophy our myths.

As ten, as twenty, now
we break from single thought
and rid of being two
receive them and walk out.

THE BANDS AND THE BEAUTIFUL CHILDREN

Band makes a tunnel of the open street
at first, hearing it;
seeing it band becomes
high: brasses ascending on the strings of sun
build their own auditorium of light,
windows from cornets
and a dome of drums.

And always attendant on bands, the beautiful children
white with running and innocence;
and the arthritic old
who, patient behind their windows
are no longer split by the quick yellow of imagination
or carried beyond their angular limits of distance.

But the children move
in the trembling building of sound,
sure as a choir
until band breaks and scatters,
crumbles about them and is made of men
tired and grumbling
on the straggling grass.

And the children, lost, lost,
in an open space,
remember the certainty of the anchored home
and cry on the unknown edge of their own city
their lips stiff from an imaginary trumpet.

ONLY CHILD

The early conflict made him pale
and when he woke from those long weeping slumbers she was
                                                    there
and the air about them—hers and his—
sometimes a comfort to him, like a quilt, but more
often than not a fear.

There were times he went away—he knew not where—
over the fields or scuffing to the shore;
suffered her eagerness on his return
for news of him—where had he been, what done?
He hardly knew, nor did he wish to know
or think about it vocally or share
his private world with her.

Then they would plan another walk, a long
adventure in the country, for her sake—
in search of birds. Perhaps they'd find the blue
heron today, for sure the kittiwake.

Birds were familiar to him now, he knew
them by their feathers and a shyness like his own
soft in the silence.
Of the ducks she said, 'Observe,
the canvas-back's a diver,' and her words
stuccoed the slaty water of the lake.

He had no wish to separate them in groups
or learn the latin,
or, waking early to their song remark, 'The thrush,'
or say at evening when the air is streaked
with certain swerving flying,
'Ah, the swifts.'

Birds were his element like air and not
her words for them—making them statues
setting them apart,
nor were they facts and details like a book.

When she said, 'Look!'
he let his eyeballs harden
and when two came and nested in the garden
he felt their softness, gentle, near his heart.

She gave him pictures which he avoided, showing
strange species flat against a foreign land.
Rather would he lie in the grass, the deep grass of the island
close to the gulls' nests knowing
these things he loved and needed near his hand,
untouched and hardly seen but deeply understood.
Or sail among them through a wet wind feeling
their wings within his blood.

Like every mother's boy he loved and hated
smudging the future photograph she had,
yet struggled within the frames of her eyes and then
froze for her, the noted naturalist—
her very affectionate and famous son.
But when most surely in her grasp, his smile
darting and enfolding her, his words:
'Without my mother's help . . .' the dream occurred.

Dozens of flying things surrounded him
on a green terrace in the sun
and one by one
as if he held caresses in his palm
he caught them all and snapped and wrung their necks
brittle as little sticks.
Then through the bald, unfeathered air
and coldly as a man would walk
against a metal backdrop, he
bore down on her
and placed them in her wide maternal lap
and accurately said their names aloud:
woodpecker, sparrow, meadowlark, nuthatch.

LITTLE GIRLS

More than discovery—rediscovery.
They renew
acquaintanceship with all things
as with flowers in dreams.

And delicate as a sketch made by being,
they merge in a singular way with their own thoughts,
drawing an arabesque with a spoon or fork
casually on the air behind their shoulders,
or talk in a confidential tone as if
their own ears held the hearing of another.

Legs in the dance go up as though on strings
pulled by their indifferent wanton hands

while anger blows into them and through their muslin
easily as sand or wind.

Older, they become round and hard, demand
shapes that are real, castles on the shore
and all the lines and angles of tradition
are mustered for them in their eagerness
to become whole, fit themselves to the thing
they see outside them,
while the thing they left
lies like a caul in some abandoned place,
unremembered by fingers or the incredibly bright
stones, which for a time replace their eyes.

SISTERS

These children split each other open like nuts,
break and crack in the small house,
are doors slamming.
Still, on the whole, are gentle for mother, take
her simple comfort like a drink of milk.

Fierce on the street they own the sun and spin
on separate axes
attract about them in their motion all
the shrieking neighbourhood of little earths,
in violence hold hatred in their mouths.

With evening their joint gentle laughter leads
them into pastures of each other's eyes;
beyond, the world is barren; they contract
tenderness from each other like disease
and talk as if each word had just been born—
a butterfly, and soft from its cocoon.

VIRGIN

By the sun, by the sudden flurry
of birds in a flock,
oh, by love's ghost
and the imagined guest—
all these
shattering, shaking the girl
in her maidenhood,
she knows
him and his green song smooth as a stone
and the word
quick with the sap and the bud and the moving bird.

BOY WITH A SEA DREAM

In his head
the masts of ships, the mists
of his own maritimes
and ancient hulls,
keels rusting where they lie
in the iodine air.
There the tall riggings of his wishes ride
and gulls like Peters blow
and slow elliptical porpoises below
his own dark waves
roll like his decks.

Unsteadying for a boy
the rock and rush
of water underfoot,
unknowns that conjure seas
from which arise
whole finely fretted archipelagoes
of coral where white flowering sea-weeds creep
to break with his high tide;
and all the deep
clear bottle green
of his ocean thought
where like a sleep
strange men drown drowsily
spiralling down the sea's steep underlip,
their lazy eyes
closed as if listening to arpeggios.

What wonder then if his geometry
become an abstract fleet
if pennants fly
pinned to the apex of each triangle?
What wonder if he lie
becalmed and idle on his bed
or if he drift
pulled by slow tides?
For like the perfect schooner which is pushed
through the slim neck to fill a bottle's shape
his dream has filled the cavern of his head
and he, a brimful seascape,
a blue brine,
with undertows and sudden swells
which toll his bells
and watery laws to be obeyed
and strange salt deaths to die.

BLOWING BOY

He is, I think, somebody else and not this
flapping and swaying apparition on strings.
Even his eyes are newly painted and not his
and I have seen his hands like a pair of old gloves
that are hungry for hands, hanging with only air
bulging the fingertips.

World is a wind about him. Everything blows.
Objects rise up and fly away like crows,
become small specks or nothing—cease to exist.
Within him there
seems to be no ballast against this air.
He spins out on a long string grown tight
and splits an acre of blue sky like a kite.

Night laps about him. In the liquid dark
all his words are released and new words find him.
Like homing pigeons come his blowing thoughts
back to roost within him. He is huge—
the burning centre of
everything, but most especially love.

Waking from dreams sometimes he is a ship
without the crew or chart to master it.
He is half master, half his master's fool
but on the corner with the boys his laugh
can halve a passing girl and make him whole.

ADOLESCENCE

In love they wore themselves in a green embrace.
A silken rain fell through the spring upon them.
In the park she fed the swans and he
whittled nervously with his strange hands.
And white was mixed with all their colours
as if they drew it from the flowering trees.

At night his two-finger whistle brought her down
the waterfall stairs to his shy smile
which, like an eddy, turned her round and round
lazily and slowly so her will
was nowhere—as in dreams things are and aren't.

Strolling along avenues in the dark
street lamps sang like sopranos in their heads
with a violence they never understood
and all their movements when they were together
had no conclusion.

Only leaning into the question had they motion;
after they parted were savage and swift as gulls.
Asking and asking the hostile emptiness
they were as sharp as partly sculptured stone
and all who watched, forgetting, were amazed
to see them form and fade before their eyes.

YOUNG GIRLS

Nothing, not even fear of punishment
can stop the giggle in a girl.
Oh mothers' trim
shapes on the chesterfield cannot dispel
their lolloping fatness.
Adolescence tumbles about in them
on cinder schoolyard or behind the expensive gates.

See them in class like porpoises
with smiles and tears
loosed from the same subterranean faucet; some
find individual adventure in
the obtuse angle, some in a phrase
that leaps like a smaller fish from a sea of words.
But most, deep in their daze, dawdle and roll,
their little breasts like wounds beneath their clothes.

A shoal of them in a room makes it a pool.
How can one teacher keep the water out,
or, being adult, find the springs and taps
of their tempers and tortures?
Who on a field filled with their female cries
can reel them in on a line of words
or land them neatly in a net?
On the dry ground they goggle, flounder, flap.

Too much weeping in them and unfamiliar blood
has set them perilously afloat.
Not divers these—but as if the waters rose in flood—
making them partially amphibious
and always drowning a little and hearing bells;
until the day the shore line wavers less,
and caught and swung on the bright hooks of their sex,
earth becomes home, their natural element.

MORNING, NOON AND NIGHT

The season of self-pity and of flowers
is here again—
the fine-boned perilous girls
are sprigged with little bows
oh hey ho nonny.

From their moist sleep arising they are great
areas of hot skin and of heart;
trot and clip to work like ponies nobbed
with coloured bow and bobbin for the show—
their hair in manes
and shaggy on their shins.

Dropped from some great height they flop at noon
liquid and lazy with the heat upon
the bright green grass beneath the trees, between
the grey of public stone;
and hardly know their wish
and hardly guess
themselves as more than surface indolence.

Become at night like spikenard and stress
under the hunter's green of hanging leaves;
among the flowering street lamps they are white
and wildly wandering and light
lances their pale and simple eyes.
                           They move
caught up in eddying water—
they are slow
and urgent and unknowable as moons.

CULLEN

Cullen renounced his cradle at fifteen,
set the thing rocking with his vanishing foot
hoping the artifice would lessen the shock.
His feet were tender as puff-balls on the stones.

He explored the schools first and didn't understand
the factory-made goods they stuffed in his mind
or why the gramophone voice always ran down
before it reached the chorus of its song.
Corridors led 'from' but never 'to',
stairs were merely an optical illusion,
in the damp basement where they hung their coats
he cried with anger and was called a coward.
He didn't understand why they were taught
life was good by faces that said it was not.
He discovered early 'the writing on the wall'
was dirty words scrawled in the shadowy hall.

Cullen wrote a note on his plate with the yolk of his egg
saying he hardly expected to come back,
and then, closing his textbooks quietly
he took his personal legs into the city.
Toured stores and saw the rats beneath the counters
(he visited the smartest shopping centres)
saw the worm's bald head rise in clerks' eyes
and metal lips spew out fantasies.
Heard the time clock's tune and the wage's pardon,
saw dust in the store-room swimming towards the light
in the enormous empty store at night;
young heads fingering figures and floating freights
from hell to hell with no margin for mistakes.

Cullen bent his eye and paid a price
to sit on the mountain of seats like edelweiss—
watched the play pivot, discovered his escape
and with the final curtain went backstage;
found age and sorrow were an application,
beauty a mirage, fragrance fictionary,

the ball dress crumpled, sticky with grease and sweat.
He forgot to close the stage door as he went.

He ploughed the city, caught on a neon sign,
heard the noise of machines talking to pulp,
found the press treacherous as a mountain climb:
all upper case required an alpenstock.
Tried out the seasons then, found April cruel—
there had been no Eliot in his books at school—
discovered that stitch of knowledge on his own
remembering all the springs he had never known.
Summer grew foliage to hide the scar,
bore leaves that looked as light as tissue paper
leaves that weighed as heavy as a plate.
Fall played a flute and stuck it in his ear,
Christmas short-circuited and fired a tree
with lights and baubles; hid behind Christ; unseen
counted its presents on an adding-machine.

Cullen renounced the city, nor did he bother
to leave his door ajar for his return;
found his feet willing and strangely slipping like adders
away from the dreadful town.
Decided country, which he had never seen
was carillon greenness lying behind the eyes
and ringing the soft warm flesh behind the knees;
decided that country people were big and free.
Found himself lodgings with fishermen on a cliff,
slung his hammock from these beliefs and slept.
Morning caught his throat when he watched the men
return at dawn like silver-armoured Vikings
to women malleable as rising bread.
At last, the environment was to his liking.
Sea was his mirror and he saw himself
twisted as rope and fretted with the ripples;
concluded quietness would comb him out:
for once, the future managed to be simple.

He floated a day in stillness, felt the grass
grow in his arable body, felt the gulls
trace the tributaries of his heart and pass
over his river beds from feet to skull.
He settled with evening like a softening land
withdrew his chair from the sun the oil lamp made,
content to rest within his personal shade.
The women, gathering, tatted with their tongues
shrouds for their absent neighbours and the men
fired with lemon extract and boot-legged rum
suddenly grew immense.
No room could hold them—he was overrun,
trampled by giants, his grass was beaten down.
Nor could his hammock bear him for it hung
limp from a single nail, salty as kelp.

Cullen evacuated overnight,
he knew no other region to explore;
discovered it was nineteen thirty-nine
and volunteered at once and went to war
wondering what on earth he was fighting for.
He knew there was a reason but couldn't find it
and marched to battle half an inch behind it.

POEM IN WAR TIME

Let us by paradox
choose a Catholic close
for innocence,
wince at the smell
of beaded flowers
like rosaries on a bush.
Let us stand together then
till the cool evening
settles this silent place
and having seen the hatted priest
walk with book from presbytery to border
and the pale nuns, handless as seals,
move in the still shadow,
let us stand here close,
for death is common as grass beyond an ocean
and, with all Europe pricking in our eyes,
suddenly remember Guernica
and be gone.

GENERATION

Schooled in the rubber bath,
promoted to scooter
early, to evade and dart;
learning our numbers
adequately, with a riveting tongue;
freed from the muddle of sex
by the never-mention method
and treading
the treacherous tight-rope
of unbelieved religion,
we reached the dreadful
opacity of adolescence.

We were an ignored
and undeclared ultimatum
of solid children;
moving behind our flesh
like tumblers on the lawn
of an unknown future,
taking no definite shape—
shifting and merging
with an agenda
of unanswerable questions
growing like roots.

Tragically, Spain was our spade;
we dug at night;
the flares went up in the garden.
Walking down country lanes
we committed arson—
firing our parent-pasts;
on the wooded lands
our childhood games grew real:

police and robbers
held unsmiling faces
against each other.

We strapped our hands in slings
fearing the dreaded
gesture of compromise;
became a war;
knew love roll from a bolt
long as the soil
and, loving, saw
eyes like our own
studding the map like cities.

Now we touch continents
with our little fingers,
swim distant seas
and walk on foreign streets
wearing crash helmets
of permanent beliefs.

SOME THERE ARE FEARLESS

In streets where pleasure grins
and the bowing waiter
turns double somersaults to the table for two
and the music of the violin is a splinter
pricking the poultice of flesh; where glinting glass
shakes with falsetto laughter,
Fear, the habitué, ignores the menu
and plays with the finger bowl at his permanent table.

Tune in the ear: in tub, in tube, in cloister
he is the villain; underneath the bed,
bare-shanked and shaking; drunken in pubs; or teaching
geography to half a world of children.

In times like these, in streets like these, in alleys,
he is the master and they run for shelter
like ants to ant hills when he lifts his rattle.
While dreaming wishful dreams that will be real,
some there are, fearless, touching a distant thing—
the ferreting sun, the enveloping shade, the attainable spring,
and the wonderful soil, nameless, beneath their feet.

NO FLOWERS

You who have floated on bored water among the islands,
who have stopped for the length of a highball, the length of a tea,
at ports you cannot remember or only remember
by the shape of the sandwiches and cocktail napkins;
you who have always cruised on the luxury liner,
do you find comfort in the tiled bathrooms on this sea?

You have faithfully tipped the stewards but will they serve you
with equal faithfulness when the ship is sinking?
The steamer rug and the deck-chair in the sun
are little to cling to when the deck creaks down.
No hand-made shoes can reincarnate Peter
and Elizabeth Arden cannot withstand salt water.
Your face under the wave will be
pitiful as the little lackey's
and the initialled suitcase you pack and save
will only precipitate the gall-green grave.

There will be no laying out on the shell-ribbed bed;
no undertaker with fat white breath
to comb the feather hair or stick the pin
into the gilt-edged stock beneath the chin;
and no old woman will come with guttering hands
to seal your eyes with pennies and no old man
will need to press the tired ball of his foot
sharp on the spade to dig the hallowed spot.

Octopus arms will hold you and sea snails
will stud the lobes of your ears;
the wide blade of the water will pare your hips
down to a size sixteen—the coveted size;
and starfish, swept by wakes of other ships,
will cast their angular shapes across your eyes.

THE STENOGRAPHERS

After the brief bivouac of Sunday,
their eyes, in the forced march of Monday to Saturday,
hoist the white flag, flutter in the snow-storm of paper,
haul it down and crack in the mid-sun of temper.

In the pause between the first draft and the carbon
they glimpse the smooth hours when they were children—
the ride in the ice-cart, the ice-man's name,
the end of the route and the long walk home;

remember the sea where floats at high tide
were sea marrows growing on the scatter-green vine
or spools of grey toffee, or wasps' nests on water;
remember the sand and the leaves of the country.

Bell rings and they go and the voice draws their pencil
like a sled across snow; when its runners are frozen
rope snaps and the voice then is pulling no burden
but runs like a dog on the winter of paper.

Their climates are winter and summer—no wind
for the kites of their hearts—no wind for a flight;
a breeze at the most, to tumble them over
and leave them like rubbish—the boy-friends of blood.

In the inch of the noon as they move they are stagnant.
The terrible calm of the noon is their anguish;
the lip of the counter, the shapes of the straws
like icicles breaking their tongues, are invaders.

Their beds are their oceans—salt water of weeping
the waves that they know—the tide before sleep;
and fighting to drown they assemble their sheep
in columns and watch them leap desks for their fences
and stare at them with their own mirror-worn faces.

In the felt of the morning the calico-minded,
sufficiently starched, insert papers, hit keys,
efficient and sure as their adding machines;
yet they weep in the vault, they are taut as net curtains
stretched upon frames. In their eyes I have seen
the pin men of madness in marathon trim
race round the track of the stadium pupil.

TYPISTS

They without message, having read
the running words on their machines,
know every letter as a stamp
cutting the stencils of their ears.
Deep in their hands, like pianists,
all longing gropes and moves, is trapped
behind the tensile gloves of skin.

Or blind, sit with their faces locked
away from work. Their varied eyes
are stiff as everlasting flowers.
While fingers on a different plane
perform the automatic act
as questions grope along the dark
and twisting corridors of brain.

Crowded together typists touch
softly as ducks and seem to sense
each others' anguish with the swift
sympathy of the deaf and dumb.

PRESENTATION

Now most miraculously the most junior clerk
becomes a hero.
Oh, beautiful child
projected suddenly to executive grandeur,
gone up like an angel in the air of good wishes,
the gift and the speeches.

Dry as chalk from your files you come, unfolding.
In the hothouse they have made of their hearts
you flower
and by a double magic, force their flower—
the gift repaid in the symbol of desire.
You have become quite simply glorious.
They by comparison cannot be less.

Oh, lighted by this dream, the office glows
brightly among the double row of desks.
This day shines in their breasts like emeralds,
their faces wake from sleeping as you smile.
They have achieved new grace because you leave.
Each, at this moment, has a home, has love.

SUMMER RESORT

They lie on beaches and are proud to tan—
climb banks in search of flowers for their hair,
change colours like chameleons and seem
indolent and somehow flat and sad.

Search out the trees for love, the beach umbrellas,
the bar, the dining-room; flash as they walk,
are pretty-mouthed and careful as they talk;
send picture post-cards to their offices
brittle with ink and soft with daily phrases.

Find Sunday empty without churches—loll
not yet unwound in deck chair and by pool,
cannot do nothing neatly, while in lap,
periscope ready, scan the scene for love.

Under the near leaves or the sailing water
eyes hoist flags and handkerchiefs between the breasts,
        alive,
flutter like pallid bats at the least eddy.

Dread the return which magnifies the want—
wind in high places soaring round the heart
and carried like a starfish in a pail
through dunes and fields and lonely mountain paths.

But memory, which is thinner than the senses,
is only a wave in grass that the kiss erases,
and love, once found, their metabolism changes:
the kiss is worn like a badge upon the mouth—
pinned there in darkness, emphasized in daylight.

Now all the scene is flying. Before the face
people and trees are swift; the enormous pool
brims like a crying eye. The immediate flesh
is real and night no curtain.

There, together, the swift exchange of badges
accelerates to a personal prize giving
while pulse and leaf rustle and grow climactic.

THE LANDLADY

Through sepia air the boarders come and go,
impersonal as trains. Pass silently
the craving silence swallowing her speech;
click doors like shutters on her camera eye.

Because of her their lives become exact:
their entrances and exits are designed;
phone calls are cryptic. Oh, her ticklish ears
advance and fall back stunned.

Nothing is unprepared. They hold the walls
about them as they weep or laugh. Each face
is dialled to zero publicly. She peers
stippled with curious flesh;

pads on the patient landing like a pulse,
unlocks their keyholes with the wire of sight,
searches their rooms for clues when they are out,
pricks when they come home late.

Wonders when they are quiet, jumps when they move,
dreams that they dope or drink, trembles to know
the traffic of their brains, jaywalks their street
in clumsy shoes.

Yet knows them better than their closest friends:
their cupboards and the secrets of their drawers,
their books, their private mail, their photographs
are theirs and hers.

Knows when they wash, how frequently their clothes
go to the cleaners, what they like to eat,
their curvature of health, but even so
is not content.

And like a lover must know all, all, all.
Prays she may catch them unprepared at last
and palm the dreadful riddle of their skulls—
hoping the worst.

PARANOID

He loved himself too much. As a child was god.
Thunder stemmed from his whims,
flowers were his path.
Throughout those early days his mother was all love,
a warm projection of him
like a second heart.

In adolescence, dark and silent, he was perfect;
still godlike and like a god
cast the world out.
Crouching in his own torso as in a chapel
the stained glass of his blood
glowed in the light.

Remained a god. Each year he grew more holy
and more wholly himself.
The self spun
thinner and thinner like a moon forming
slowly from that other self
the dead sun.

Until he was alone, revolved in ether
light years from the world,
cold and remote.
Thinking he owned the heavens too, he circled,
wanly he turned and whirled
reflecting light.

MAN WITH ONE SMALL HAND

One hand is smaller than the other. It
must always be loved a little like a child;
requires attention constantly, implies
it needs his frequent glance to nurture it.

He holds it sometimes with the larger one
as adults lead a child across the street.
Finding it his or suddenly alien
rallies his interest and his sympathy.

Sometimes you come upon him unawares
just quietly staring at it where it lies
as mute and somehow perfect as a flower.

But no. It is not perfect. He admits
it has its faults: it is not strong or quick.
At night it vanishes to reappear
in dreams full-size, lost or surrealist.

Yet has its place like memory or a dog—
is never completely out of mind—a rod
to measure all uncertainties against.

Perhaps he loves it too much, sets too much stock
simply in its existence. Ah, but look!
It has its magic. See how it will fit
so sweetly, sweetly in the infant's glove.

PUPPETS

See them joined by strings to history:
their strange progenitors all born full-grown,
ancestors buried with the ancient Greeks—
slim terra-cotta dolls with articulate limbs
lying like corpses.
                              Puppets in Rome
subject to papal law, discreet in tights.

And see the types perpetuate themselves
freed from the picket prejudice of race:
the seaside Punch with his inherited nose
carried from Pulcinella round the globe
ends up in Bexhill, enters English eyes.

While here in a Sunday drawing-room beside
the bland Pacific and its rain come two
emerging full-grown from their dark cocoons—
two whose blasé antecedents once
performed for Pepys's mistress, or, in silk,
were bawdy for bored royalty at court;
escaped and raided country fairs and spread
the world with areas of Lilliput.

Before our eyes the twelve-inch clown grows large
and dances on his rubber feet and kicks
pneumatic legs, thumbs his enormous nose;
lies down for push-ups—and, exhibitionist—
suddenly turns and waves.
More clown than clowns he is all laughter, is
buoyed by it and brilliant in its light.
Unlike his living prototype has no
dichotomy to split him: this is all.
He calls your laughter out without reserve—
is only and always feet and a vulgar streak
and his music, brass.

The negro does a tap dance and his toes
click on the parquet.
Music moves in him and explodes in his toes
and somehow he is two-fold, though he grins
his hands are stripped of humour,
they are long
and lonely attached to him.

He is himself and his own symbol,
sings
terribly without a voice, is so
gentle it seems that his six delicate strings
are ropes upon him.
But still he grins, he grins.

Oh, coming isolated from their plays but not
isolated from their history,
shaped and moulded by heredity,
negro and clown in microcosm, these
small violent people shake the quiet room
and bring all history tumbling about
a giant audience that almost weeps.

JOURNEY HOME

Certainly there had been nothing but the extraordinary rain for
$\qquad\qquad\qquad\qquad\qquad\qquad\qquad\qquad\qquad$ a long time—
nothing but the rain, the grey buildings, the grey snow,
when landscape broke the lens and smacked his face
with a flag of blue
and the white thunder of snow
rolling the hills.

Hurry was in his veins;
violence vaulted the loose-box of his head;
hurry was hot in the straw
and snapped in the eyes
of the innocent traveller.

And flex and flux were there
like acrobats
waving their banners.
So declamatory was his blood
that he owned the train;
its whistle was in his throat,
its wheels in his brain.

Once he became a panoramic view,
the white of the valleys and hills
his own still flesh.
But speed re-formed him
he was forced to change
his contours and his outlook and his range.
Rushing through forest he was dark again
and the great coniferous branches brushed his face.

Rabbit spoor resembled his memory
of what he once had been—faint against faintness,
definite as dust,

of the no-taste of wafers, of the warmth
that neither gives nor takes.
Past was a pastel rubbed as he hurried past.

And now that the tunnel of trees was done, his eyes
sprinted the plain where house lights in the dusk
fired pistols for the race that led him on.
He shed the train like a snake its skin; he dodged
the waiting camera which with a simple click
could hold him fast to the spot beside the track.

And as the air inflated his lungs he stood
there in the dark at his destination knowing
somewhere—to left? to right?—he was walking home
and his shoulders were light and white as though wings were
growing.

PHOTOS OF A SALT MINE

How innocent their lives look,
how like a child's
dream of caves and winter, both combined;
the steep descent to whiteness
and the stope
with its striated walls
their folds all leaning as if pointing to
the greater whiteness still,
that great white bank
with its decisive front,
that seam upon a slope,
salt's lovely ice.

And wonderful underfoot the snow of salt
the fine
particles a broom could sweep,
one thinks
muckers might make angels in its drifts
as children do in snow,
lovers in sheets,
lie down and leave imprinted where they lay
a feathered creature holier than they.

And in the outworked stopes
with lamps and ropes
up miniature matterhorns
the miners climb
probe with their lights
the ancient folds of rock—
syncline and anticline—
and scoop from darkness an Aladdin's cave:
rubies and opals glitter from its walls.

But hoses douse the brilliance of these jewels,
melt fire to brine.
Salt's bitter water trickles thin and forms,
slow fathoms down,
a lake within a cave,
lacquered with jet—
white's opposite.
There grey on black the boating miners float
to mend the stays and struts of that old stope
and deeply underground
their words resound,
are multiplied by echo, swell and grow
and make a climate of a miner's voice.

So all the photographs like children's wishes
are filled with caves or winter,
innocence
has acted as a filter,
selected only beauty from the mine.
Except in the last picture,
it is shot
from an acute high angle. In a pit
figures the size of pins are strangely lit
and might be dancing but you know they're not.
Like Dante's vision of the nether hell
men struggle with the bright cold fires of salt,
locked in the black inferno of the rock:
the filter here, not innocence but guilt.

ELECTION DAY

I

I shut the careful door of my room and leave
letters, photographs and the growing poem—
the locked zone of my tight and personal thought
slough off—recede from down the green of the street.
Naked almost among the trees and wet—
a strike for lightning.

And everything rushes at me either fierce or friendly
in a sudden world of bulls.
Faces on posters in the leaves call out
the violent yes or no to my belief.
Are quick or slow or halted to my pulse.

Oh on this beautiful day, the weather wooing
the senses and the feel of walking
smooth in my summer legs
I lope through the tall and trembling grass and call
the streaming banner of my public colour.

II

Here in this place, the box and private privet
denote the gentleman and shut him in—
for feudally he lives and the feud on.
Colonel Evensby with his narrow feet
will cast his blue blood ballot for the Tory.

And in the polling station I shall meet
the smiling rather gentle overlords
propped by their dames and almost twins in tweeds
and mark my x against them and observe
my ballot slip, a bounder, in the box.

And take my route again through lazy streets
alive with all-out blossoming, through trees
that stint no colour for their early summer
and past an empty lot where an old dog
appoints himself as guardian of the green.

III

Radio owns my room as the day ends.
The slow returns begin, the voices call
the yes's and the no's that ring or toll;
the districts all proclaim themselves in turn
and public is my room, not personal.

Midnight. I wander on the quiet street,
its green swamped by the dark; a pale glow
sifts from the distant lamps. Behind the leaves
the faces on the posters wait and blow
tattered a little and less urgent now.

I pass the empty lot. The old dog
has trotted off to bed. The neighbourhood
is neatly hedged with privet still, the lights
are blinking off in the enormous homes.
Gentlemen, for the moment, you may sleep.

IF IT WERE YOU

If it were you, say, you
who scanning the personal map one day knew
your sharp eyes water and grow colour blind,
unable to distinguish green from blue
and everything terribly run together as if rain
had smudged the markings on the paper—
a child's painting after a storm—
and the broad avenue erased,
the landmarks gone;
and you, bewildered—not me this time and not
the cold unfriendly neighbour or the face in the news—
who walked a blind circle in a personal place;

and if you became lost, say, on the lawn,
unable to distinguish left from right
and that strange longitude that divides the body
sharply in half—that line that separates
so that one hand could never be the other—
dissolved and both your hands were one,
then in the garden though birds went on with their
                singing
and on the ground
flowers wrote their signatures in coloured ink—
would you call help like a woman assaulted,
cry to be found?

No ears would understand. Your friends and you
would be practically strangers, there would be no face
more familiar than this unfamiliar place
and there would be walls of air, invisible, holding
you single and directionless in space.

First you would be busy as a woodsman marking
the route out, making false starts and then
remembering yesterday when it was easy
you would grow lazy.
Summer would sit upon you then as on a stone
and you would be tense for a time beneath the morning sun

but always lonely
and birds perhaps would brush your coat and become
angels of deliverance
for a moment only;
clutching their promising wings you would discover
they were illusive and gone
as the lost lover.
Would you call Ariel, Ariel, in the garden,
in a dream within a dream be Orpheus
and for a certain minute take a step
delicately across the grass?

If so, there would be no answer nor reply
and not one coming forward from the leaves.
No bird nor beast with a challenging look
or friendly.
Simply nothing but you and the green garden,
you and the garden.

And there you might stay forever, mechanically
occupied, but if you raised your head
madness would rush at you from the shrubbery
or the great sun, stampeding through the sky
would stop and drop—
a football in your hands
and shrink as you watched it
to a small dark dot
forever escaping focus
like the injury to the cornea which darts
hard as a cinder across the sight but dims
fading into the air like a hocus-pocus
the minute that you are aware
and stare at it.

Might you not, if it were you,
bewildered, broken,
slash your own wrists, commit
an untidy murder in the leafy lane

and scar the delicate air with your cries or sit
weeping, weeping in the public square
your flimsy butterfly fingers in your hair
your face destroyed by rain?

If it were you, the person you call 'I',
the one you loved and worked for,
the most high
now become Ishmael,
might you not
grow phobias about calendars and clocks,
stare at your face in the mirror, not knowing it
and feel an identity with idiots and dogs
as all the exquisite unborns of your dreams
deserted you to snigger behind their hands?

NOW THIS COLD MAN . . .

Now this cold man in his garden feels the ice
thawing from branches of his lungs and brain:
the blood thins out in artery and vein,
the stiff eyes slip again.

Kneeling in welters of narcissus his
dry creaking joints bend with a dancer's ease,
the roughened skin softens beneath the rain

and all that he had clutched, held tightly locked
behind the fossil frame
dissolves, flows free
in saffron covering the willow tree
and coloured rivers of the rockery.

Yellow and white and purple is his breath
his hands are curved and cool for cupping petals,
the sharp green shoots emerging from the beds
all whistle for him

until he is the garden; heart, the sun
and all his body soil;
glistening jonquils blossom from his skull,
the bright expanse of lawn his stretching thighs
and something rare and perfect, yet unknown,
stirs like a foetus just behind his eyes.

STORIES OF SNOW

Those in the vegetable rain retain
an area behind their sprouting eyes
held soft and rounded with the dream of snow
precious and reminiscent as those globes—
souvenir of some never-nether land—
which hold their snow-storms circular, complete,
high in a tall and teakwood cabinet.

In countries where the leaves are large as hands
where flowers protrude their fleshy chins
and call their colours,
an imaginary snow-storm sometimes falls
among the lilies.
And in the early morning one will waken
to think the glowing linen of his pillow
a northern drift, will find himself mistaken
and lie back weeping.
And there the story shifts from head to head,
of how in Holland, from their feather beds
hunters arise and part the flakes and go
forth to the frozen lakes in search of swans—
the snow-light falling white along their guns,
their breath in plumes.
While tethered in the wind like sleeping gulls
ice-boats wait the raising of their wings
to skim the electric ice at such a speed
they leap jet strips of naked water,
and how these flying, sailing hunters feel
air in their mouths as terrible as ether.
And on the story runs that even drinks
in that white landscape dare to be no colour;
how flasked and water clear, the liquor slips
silver against the hunters' moving hips.
And of the swan in death these dreamers tell
of its last flight and how it falls, a plummet,
pierced by the freezing bullet

and how three feathers, loosened by the shot,
descend like snow upon it.
While hunters plunge their fingers in its down
deep as a drift, and dive their hands
up to the neck of the wrist
in that warm metamorphosis of snow
as gentle as the sort that woodsmen know
who, lost in the white circle, fall at last
and dream their way to death.

And stories of this kind are often told
in countries where great flowers bar the roads
with reds and blues which seal the route to snow—
as if, in telling, raconteurs unlock
the colour with its complement and go
through to the area behind the eyes
where silent, unrefractive whiteness lies.

CHRISTMAS EVE—MARKET SQUARE

City of Christmas, here, I love your season,
where in the market square,
bristled and furry
like a huge animal
the fir trees lie
silently waiting buyers.
    It's as if
    they hold the secrets of a Christmas sealed—
    as statues hold their feelings sealed in stone—
    to burst in bells and baubles on their own
    within the warmth and lightness of a house.

The sellers, bunched and bundled,
hold their ears,
blow lazy boas as they call their wares,
and children out of legends pulling sleds,
prop tall trees straight in search of symmetry
and haul their spikey aromatic wonder
home through a snowy world.
    Almost the tree sings through them in their carols
    almost grows taller in their torsos, is
    perfectly theirs, as nothing ever was.

The soft snow falls,
vague smiling drunkards weave
gently as angels through a street of feathers;
balancing bulging parcels with their wings
they tip-toe where the furry monster grows
smaller and hoarier
and nerveless sprawls
flat on its mammoth, unimagined face.
    While in far separate houses
    all its nerves
    spring up like rockets,
    unknown children see
    a miracle
    and cry
    to cut the ceiling not to lop the tree.

SLEEPER

The ritual of bedtime takes its shape
meadowed with sheets and hilled with pillows plumped
for head's indenture—
oh, the prairie air's plangent with scent of soap.

Now, silken, smooth, the body stretches out
easy with sleep;
beneath the lazy hand
print that the eye has sprinted on grows fur
to stroke a milky eye.

Light goes with an explosion.
In the head
colours remain like ribbons—
drift and blow;
move and are static, fill a floating frame,
flow over and reform in fern and sand.

The gentle dreamer drowns without a sound
softly in eiderdown.
Almost, he dies.
As divers who are dead, his body floats
pneumatic on black tides.

Complete in sleep, discards his arms and legs
with only whimpers;
from his flesh retreats
like water through a mesh, leaving it beached
alone upon a bed.

And takes the whole night in his lungs and head.
A hydrocephalic idiot, quick at sums
wandering strangely lost and loose among
symbols as blunted and as bright as flowers.

NIGHTMARE

In the white bed
this too-dark creature nests,
litters her yelping young
upon my breasts.

Dreams are her thicket
in them wearing masks
of my familiar faces
she dissembles.

Trembles in every image
calls my falcon
which falls, a feathered stone
to her white wrist bone.

Twists me like wire,
stretches me tight and thin,
a black skeleton stark
among flowering apples.

Or, an appalling valentine
of lace and hearts
hot and frilled,
abandoned in the sun

do I become
at the dark bitter wish
of this night-walking
anxious alchemist.

Sometimes she smiles at me
as if I were
her own face
smiling in a mirror

and she rehearsing
sweet looks in my eyes
of barley sugar
and of butterflies.

Yet should I sleep forever
she would eat
my beating heart
as if it were a plum

did she not know
with terrible wisdom
by doing so
she would devour her own.

REFLECTION IN A TRAIN WINDOW

There is a woman floating in a window—
transparent—
Christmas wreaths in passing houses
shine now in eye and now in hair, in heart.
How like a saint with visions, the stigmata
marking her like a martyr.

Merged with a background of mosaic
she drifts
through tenement transoms, independent stars,
while in between her and herself the sharp
frost crystals prick the pane with thorns.

She without substance, ectoplasmic, still,
is haloed with the reading lamps of strangers
while brass and brick pass through her.
                                    Yet she stirs
to some soft soundless grieving and tears well
in her unseeing eyes and from the sill
her trembling image falls, rises and falls.

VEGETABLE ISLAND

Flowers own it.
Everywhere their flags flutter.
The deep woods are stormed
and trees throw bouquets to each other, pass
petals along from bough to bough.
It is theirs.

There is no window they have not invaded,
pressed or crept over the sill of, flung
their scent like a symbol through an entire room.
Business men in offices, dictating,
smelling the hanging baskets from the streets
stop and wonder about their gardens, ponder
are they too lush and lovely lovely are they
a little out of hand? The hedges calling
coyly as they advance,
the bright grass
silently leaping.

Sometimes a man must seek the sea out here.
Down where small lichens stucco all the rocks
it smacks with a smell of chowder on the shore.
A cormorant with periscope neck floats black
among the gulls. Some bird in tiny ambush stamps about,
undoes the sudden buzzer in its throat,
and breaks the sweetness of the simmering gorse.
Oh, undiseased by pollen, hand in water
beneath the saline wave is sharp and clear
unsmudged by pastel petal, uncorrupted.

Sometimes a man must strip and throw his body
into the acid ocean to erase
the touch and scent of flowers, their little cries
like sickly mistresses, their gentle faces
pleading consumption.
Sometimes he has no strength to meet a tree
debauched with blossoms.

But women wander unafraid as if
they made the petals
and tiny children in the meadows wave
with wildflowers in their fists
or strip the woods of flowers
and turn away
to fresh and unrelated interests
as if the flesh were only hurt by what
is made of metal—knife-blade or buckshot.

PORTRAIT OF MARINA

Far out the sea has never moved. It is
Prussian forever, rough as teazled wool
some antique skipper worked into a frame
to bear his lost four-master.
                              Where it hangs
now in a sunny parlour, none recalls
how all his stitches, interspersed with oaths
had made his one pale spinster daughter grow
transparent with migraines—and how his call
fretted her more than waves.
                              Her name
Marina, for his youthful wish—
boomed at the font of that small salty church
where sailors lurched like drunkards—would, he felt
make her a water woman, rich with bells.
To her the name Marina simply meant
he held his furious needle for her thin
fingers to thread again with more blue wool
to sew the ocean of his memory.
Now, where the picture hangs, a dimity
young inland housewife with inherited
clocks under bells and ostrich eggs on shelves
pours amber tea in small rice china cups
and reconstructs
how great-great-grandpapa at ninety-three
his fingers knotted with arthritis, his
old eyes grown agatey with cataracts
became as docile as a child again—
that fearful salty man—
and sat, wrapped round in faded paisley shawls
gently embroidering.
While Aunt Marina in grey worsted, warped
without a smack of salt, came to his call
the sole survivor of his last shipwreck.

* * *

Slightly off shore it glints. Each wave is capped
with broken mirrors. Like Marina's head
the glinting of these waves.
She walked forever antlered with migraines
her pain forever putting forth new shoots
until her strange unlovely head became
a kind of candelabra—delicate—
where all her tears were perilously hung
and caught the light as waves that catch the sun.
The salt upon the panes, the grains of sand
that crunched beneath her heel
her father's voice, 'Marina!'—all these broke
her trembling edifice. The needle shook
like ice between her fingers.
In her head
too many mirrors dizzied her and broke.

* * *

But where the wave breaks, where it rises green
turns into gelatin, becomes a glass
simply for seeing stones through, runs across
the coloured shells and pebbles of the shore
and makes an aspic of them
then sucks back
in foam and undertow—
this aspect of the sea
Marina never knew.

For her the sea was Father's Fearful Sea
harsh with sea serpents
winds and drowning men.
For her it held no spiral of a shell
for her descent to dreams,
it held no bells.
And where it moved in shallows it was more
imminently a danger, more alive
than where it lay off shore full fathom five.

IN A SHIP RECENTLY RAISED FROM THE SEA

Bright fish once swimming where we lie
lazy upon this bunk,
quicksilvered the fluid sheets
moved in a maze of mirrors.
The mackerel eye, the liquid fin
swam in the curve your arm is making.

All tilting then, a dome of tears
trembled and settled on the silt.
Where women wept in mercury
a school of pewter shadows traced
parabolas upon the linen
which once had wrapped their lilyskin.

Rinsed now in parables of waves,
by half sleep lapped and locked
and wimpled in this shifting space
your face rocks in my water self,
awash as when fish slanted in
the enclave of this briny cabin.

THE FLOWER AND THE ROCK

She felt the flower of his pain beneath her hand
which cupped for it and was soft and yearned as if
all her blood had withdrawn to the stamping wrist
and her hand was wax, wanting the pain in it
so that it came, incised and exquisite
as the fossil of fern or a delicate hairy plant
which almost lived, almost uncurled and bloomed
perishably and purely in her palm.

While he felt only the solid rock of pain
crack to receive the violence of the sword
whenever she came or asked or said his name.

LOVE POEM

Remembering you and reviewing
our structural love
the past re-arises alive
from its smothering dust.

For memory which is only decadent
in hands like a miser's
loving the thing for its thingness,
or in the eyes of collectors who assess
the size, the incredible size, of their collection,
can, in the living head, create and make
new the sometimes appallingly ancient present
and sting the sleeping thing
to a sudden seeing.

And as a tree with all its leaves relaxed
shivers at the memory of wind
or the still waters of a pool recall
their springing origin and rise and fall
suddenly over the encircling basin's lip—
so I, remembering from now to then
can know and see and feel again, as jewels
must when held in a brilliant branch of sun.

PHOTOGRAPH

They are all beneath the sea in this photograph—
not dead surely—merely a little muted:
those two lovers lying apart and stiff
with a buoy above which could ring their beautiful
     movements;

and she with the book, reading as through a bowl
words that were never written, f's like giraffes
and vowels distorted and difficult as code
which make her lazily turn away and laugh;

he with hands so pale they might be dying
sits with paints and paper painting sand
and wears a skin of corrugated water
which stillness opens on his sea-scape mind.

And all their paraphernalia a pretense:
cigarettes, matches, cameras and dark glasses
and the pair of water wings which refuse to float
are idle in their submarine oasis.

While overhead the swimmers level waves,
shrinking the distance between continents
and closer inland from the broken weirs
the fishermen are hauling giant nets.

MINERAL

Soft and unmuscular among the flowers and papers
and changed as if grown deaf or slightly lame
she writes to strangers about him as if he were a stranger,
avoids the name
which he no longer has a use for, which
he disinherited as he was leaving.
It had a different ring when he was living.

Now he is mineral to her. In a game
she would declare him mineral without thinking.
Mineral his going and his having gone
and on her desk, his photo—mineral.

No gentle mirage loves her as a dream
can love a person's head, no memory
comes warm and willing to her tears. She walks
nearly begonia between the walls,
calls out against an echo. Nothing's real
but mineral: cold touch, sharp taste of it
lodger forever in her routed house.

CONTAGION

Beside these streams, by wet and open lakes
where weeping willows, stripped of their leaves, are fountains
singly or in faded pairs they walk
the twisted paths beneath the dripping trees
almost as if their mouths were sealed and words
forced to parade as ghosts.

Those who have suffered from the same disease
can spot them in a minute—it's as though
they're recent exiles from a fever who,
compelled by echo,
search for the lost peaks of delirium's mountains
in a land where temperatures are low.

And re-infected by their look and by
the flat horizon and the weeping trees,
now if my lover were to come like a lion
over the muted grasses, even I
would view him for a moment with their eyes,
feel locked outside the currents he released.

THE CONDEMNED

For L. O.

In separate cells they tapped the forbidden message.
Even the wide-eared warden could never hear
their miniature conversation
though he slipped the bolt of his hearing and walked the
                                                    passage.

Then feeling the walls would dissolve with love they
        planned
the inevitable and leisurely excavation;
tap grew into chip behind the bed
as darkness hid the activities of the hand.

In an area a cigarette could light, everything lived.
The intricate machinery of the head
stopped and the heart's attention
increased the circumference of what they loved.

Then as the wall grew thin they wore their hopes
inwardly like a name they must never mention;
the riots of the skin were still to listen
for the warden's silent black-and-white approach.

And as their fingers groped and came together
it was so suddenly tender in that prison
birds might have sung from water—just as if
two mouths meeting and melting had become each other.

Later the whole hand grasped and the ultimate escape
plunging through velvet to an earth so stiff
their footfall left no mark
though their feet felt sharp, resuming use and shape.

Their lungs, in all that air, filled like balloons,
pastel and luminous against the dark:
no angels could have had more grace
in a children's heaven full of suns and moons.

But light destroyed their splendour, all their soft
movements jerked to woodcuts and the lace
of their imagination atrophied.
Their stark identities—all they had left—

were mirrored upon fence and parish hall
and plastered on the staring countryside
till each became a terror and a face
and everywhere they went was nowhere at all.

THE EVENT

The keys all turned to that event
as if it were a magnetic lock.
A rush of streams flowed into it
thundering from the great divide
while numberless and hidden heads
like flowers leaned out to feel its light.

The lion, somnolent with food,
the bear in his continuing winter,
rose to its bell as if their blood
conveyed its red and vital current.
That instant the indifferent street
became their sudden food.

Lilies and archangels began
the gradual gentling of the lion.
The burred bear fell asleep again—
a snowfall lulled him to a lamb.
Like velvet toys they lie there prone
and dream the cactus plant of pain.

But children will be born whose blood
remembers that event.
The lion and bear will waken up
ravenous after sleep
and lilies then will be their bread,
archangels their white meat.

AND WE TWO

I dreamed my most extraordinary darling
gangling, come to share
my hot and prairie childhood

the first day loosed the mare from her picket
and rode her bareback
over the little foothills towards the mountains.

And on the second, striding from his tent,
twisted a noose of butcher's string.
Ingenious to my eyes the knots he tied.

The third bright day he laid the slack noose over
the gopher's burrow,
unhurried by the chase,

and lolled a full week, lazy, in the sun
until the head popped, sleek, enquiring.
The noose pulled tight around its throat.

Then the small fur lashed, lit out, hurling
about only to turn
tame silk in his palm

as privy harness, tangled from his pocket
with leash of string
slipped simply on.

But the toy beast and the long rein and the paid out lengths
of our youth snapped
as the creature jibbed and bit

and the bright blood ran out, the bright blood trickled over,
slowed, grew dark
lay sticky on our skins.

And we two, dots upon that endless plain, Leviathan became
and filled and broke
the glass air like twin figures, vast, in stone.

THE MAP

That day we followed an idle road
away from the river and its crowds,
another direction was our intention
and our wish was simply to be alone.

We stopped the car where the Shield arose
ancient and steep from the blowing fields
and climbed to a ridge that was high and sweet,
where the leaves were low and the grass was thick.

And far away in our tent of trees
on the side of the Shield, if we could have seen
through the green of our tent, we'd have had a view
of minutely delicate blowing fields,

where strawberries hot on the ground as blood
lay in their leaves as we in ours
a world away on Precambrian rock,
where no one had ever been but us.

Yet when we arose and started back
we found we followed a well-worn track,
a gentle slope, no sharp incline
like the hill we had climbed on the journey up.

And back in town with a detail map
our fingers searched for the very spot
where we had lain in a leafy tent
pegged to the ancient, igneous rock.

And it was less than an easy mile
from the river we'd turned our backs upon,
by the map—if one could believe the scale—
and less than a stone's throw from a farm.

The map is cold with facts, we said,
and objectivity's great untruth
dissolved as our tracing fingers met
soft on the symbol for the rock.

But we were wrong and the map was true
and had we stood and looked about
from our height of land, we'd have had a view
which since, we have had to learn by heart.

THE APPLE

Look, look, he took me straight
to the snake's eye
to the striped flower
shielding its peppery root.

I said, I shall never go back.

At harvest he led me round and about.
The ground
was apple red and round.
The trees bare.
One apple only hung like a heart in air.

Together, bite by bite
we ate,
mouths opposite.
Bit clean through core and all to meet:
through sweet juice met.

I said, I shall never go back.

But someone let an angel down
on a thin string.
It was a rangey paper thing
with one wing torn,
born of a child.

Now, now, we come and go, we come and go,
feverish where that harvest grew.

T-BAR

Relentless, black on white, the cable runs
through metal arches up the mountain side.
At intervals giant pickaxes are hung
on long hydraulic springs. The skiers ride
propped by the axehead, twin automatons
supported by its handle, one each side.

In twos they move slow motion up the steep
incision in the mountain. Climb. Climb.
Somnambulists, bolt upright in their sleep
their phantom poles swung lazily behind,
while to the right, the empty T-bars keep
in mute descent, slow monstrous jigging time.

Captive the skiers now and innocent,
wards of eternity, each pair alone.
They mount the easy vertical ascent,
pass through successive arches, bride and groom,
as through successive naves, are newly wed
participants in some recurring dream.

So do they move forever. Clocks are broken.
In zones of silence they grow tall and slow,
inanimate dreamers, mild and gentle-spoken
blood-brothers of the haemophilic snow
until the summit breaks and they awaken
imagos from the stricture of the tow.

Jerked from her chrysalis the sleeping bride
suffers too sudden freedom like a pain.
The dreaming bridegroom severed from her side
singles her out, the old wound aches again.
Uncertain, lost, upon a wintry height
these two, not separate, but no longer one.

Now clocks begin to peck and sing. The slow
extended minute like a rubber band
contracts to catapult them through the snow
in tandem trajectory while behind
etching the sky-line, obdurate and slow
the spastic T-bars pivot and descend.

THE PERMANENT TOURISTS

Somnolent through landscapes and by trees
nondescript, almost anonymous,
they alter as they enter foreign cities—
the terrible tourists with their empty eyes
longing to be filled with monuments.

Verge upon statues in the public squares
remembering the promise of memorials
yet never enter the entire event
as dogs, abroad in any kind of weather,
move perfectly within their rainy climate.

Lock themselves into snapshots on the steps
of monolithic bronze as if suspecting
the subtle mourning of the photograph
might later conjure in the memory
all they are now incapable of feeling.

And search all heroes out: the boy who gave
his life to save a town; the stolid queen;
forgotten politicians minus names
and the plunging war dead, permanently brave,
forever and ever going down to death.

Look, you can see them nude in any café
reading their histories from the bill of fare,
creating futures from a foreign teacup.
Philosophies like ferns bloom from the fable
that travel is broadening at the café table.

Yet somehow beautiful, they stamp the plaza.
Classic in their anxiety they call
all sculptured immemorial stone
into their passive eyes, as rivers
draw ruined columns to their placid glass.

H's Garden

Night Garden (detail)

Mato Fino

World Within World (detail)

COOK'S MOUNTAINS

By naming them he made them.
They were there
before he came
but they were not the same.
It was his gaze
that glazed each one.
He saw
the Glass House Mountains in his glass.
They shone.

And still they shine.
We saw them as we drove—
sudden, surrealist, conical
they rose
out of the rain forest.
The driver said,
'Those are the Glass House Mountains up ahead.'

And instantly they altered to become
the sum of shape and name.
Two strangenesses united into one
more strange than either.
Neither of us now
remembers how they looked before they broke
the light to fragments as the driver spoke.

Like mounds of mica,
hive-shaped hothouses,
mountains of mirror glimmering
they form
in diamond panes behind the tree ferns of
the dark imagination,
burn and shake
the lovely light of Queensland like a bell
reflecting Cook upon a deck
his tongue
silvered with paradox and metaphor.

BARK DRAWING

This is a landscape with serifs:

singularly sharp
each emu
kangaroo &
goanna
intaglio
on the bark
of this continent

look in its rivers
fish
swim by in skeleton
fine-boned as a comb

while pin-figured men
string thin
are dancing or hunting

(an alphabet the eye
lifts from the air
as if by ear

two senses
threaded through
a knuckle bone)

stare through
sea water clear
as isinglass or air

there spirit men
giraffid
catch sting ray &
skate
zither-like

or with boomerang
bull roarer &
dilly bag

stipple the bark between
zig-zag &
herring-bone

& in ceremonial
fill the least paddock
with cross hatch &
serif.

ON EDUCATING THE NATIVES

They who can from palm leaves and from grasses
weave baskets of so intricate a beauty
and simply as a girl combing her hair,
are taught in a square room by a square woman
to cross-stitch on checked gingham.

GIOVANNI AND THE INDIANS

They call to pass the time with Giovanni
and speak an English none can understand
as Giovanni trims the weeping willow,
his ladder teetering in the yellow leaves.

They make him teeter even when he's steady;
their tatters blow and catch him through the trees;
those scraps of colour flutter against stucco
and flash like foreign birds;

and eyes look out at eyes till Giovanni's
are lowered swiftly—one among them is
perhaps the Evil Eye. The weather veers.
Pale leaves flap wetly on the metal trees.

*   *   *

Bare winter is pure glass. Past panes of air
he peers but sees no colour flicking raw
behind the little twigs; no movement shakes
the sunlight on the berries, no branch cracks

till quakes of spring unsettle them. Their flocks
emerge, they sprinkle paths with petals.
Now Giovanni pauses, stares and shrugs
hiding behind a golden blind of wattle.

*   *   *

One on a cycle, like a ragged sail
that luffs and sags, comes tacking up the hill.
Does Giovanni smile as he darts off, low
over the handle-bars of his spinning wheel?

And one, his turban folded like a jug,
and frocked, walks brittle on his blanco'd legs—
a bantam cockerel. Giovanni looks
and laughs and laughs and lurches in great loops

and stoops to bend above a bed and gather
hyacinths, tulips, waterblue and yellow;
passes his offering through the rainy willow
nodding, 'Good fellow,' smiling, 'much good fellow.'

AFTER RAIN

The snails have made a garden of green lace:
broderie anglaise from the cabbages,
chantilly from the choux-fleurs, tiny veils—
I see already that I lift the blind
upon a woman's wardrobe of the mind.

Such female whimsy floats about me like
a kind of tulle, a flimsy mesh,
while feet in gum boots pace the rectangles—
garden abstracted, geometry awash—
an unknown theorem argued in green ink,
dropped in the bath.
Euclid in glorious chlorophyll, half drunk.

I none too sober slipping in the mud
where rigged with guys of rain
the clothes-reel gauche
as the rangey skeleton of some
gaunt delicate spidery mute
is pitched as if
listening;
while hung from one thin rib
a silver web—
its infant, skeletal, diminutive,
now sagged with sequins, pulled ellipsoid,
glistening.

I suffer shame in all these images.
The garden is primeval, Giovanni
in soggy denim squelches by my hub
over his ruin,
shakes a doleful head.
But he so beautiful and diademmed,
his long Italian hands so wrung with rain
I find his ache exists beyond my rim
and almost weep to see a broken man
made subject to my whim.

O choir him, birds, and let him come to rest
within this beauty as one rests in love,
till pears upon the bough
encrusted with
small snails as pale as pearls
hang golden in
a heart that knows tears are a part of love.

And choir me too to keep my heart a size
larger than seeing, unseduced by each
bright glimpse of beauty striking like a bell,
so that the whole may toll,
its meaning shine
clear of the myriad images that still—
do what I will—encumber its pure line.

THE METAL AND THE FLOWER

Intractable between them grows
a garden of barbed wire and roses.
Burning briars like flames devour
their too innocent attire.
Dare they meet, the blackened wire
tears the intervening air.

Trespassers have wandered through
texture of flesh and petals.
Dogs like arrows moved along
pathways that their noses knew.
While the two who laid it out
find the metal and the flower
fatal underfoot.

Black and white at midnight glows
this garden of barbed wire and roses.
Doused with darkness roses burn
coolly as a rainy moon;
beneath a rainy moon or none
silver the sheath on barb and thorn.

Change the garden, scale and plan:
wall it, make it annual.
There the briary flower grew.
There the brambled wire ran.
While they sleep the garden grows,
deepest wish annuls the will:
perfect still the wire and rose.

THE KNITTERS

These women knitting knit a kind of mist—
climate of labyrinth—
into the air.
Sitting like sleepers,
propped against the chintz,
pin-headed somehow—figures by Moore—
arachnes in their webs, they barely stir—

except their eyes and hands, which wired to some
urgent personal circuit,
move as if
a switch controlled them.
Hear the click and hum
as their machines translating hieroglyphs,
compulsive and monotonous, consume—
lozenge and hank—the candy-coloured stuff.

See two observe the ceremony of skeins:
one, forearms raised,
the loops around her palms,
catscradle rocks, is metronome, becalmed;
while her companion
spun from her as from
a wooden spindle, winds a woollen world.

A man rings like an axe, is alien,
imperilled by them,
finds them cold and far.
They count their stitches on a female star
and speak another language,
are not kin.
Or is he Theseus remembering
that maze, those daedal ways, the Minotaur?

They knit him out, the wool grows thick and fills
the room they sit in like a fur
as vegetable more than animal,
surrealist and slightly sinister,
driven by motors strong beyond their wills,
these milky plants devour
more hanks of wool, more cubic feet of air.

WAR LORD IN THE EARLY EVENING

Suitable for a gentleman with medals
to choose for pleasure
and his beneficent care
the long-stemmed roses wilting in the summer weather.

Fitting for a man in his position
to succour them with water
at his side
admiring, dressed in muslin, his small daughter.

He saw the picture clearly. It was charming:
the battered war lord
in the early evening
among the roses, gentle and disarming.

The way he sent the servants for the hoses
they thought a fire was raging
in the garden.
Meanwhile the roses and the light were fading.

Six choppy lengths of tubing were assembled.
Bind them, the general stormed
from six make one.
Was this philosophy? It wasn't plumbing.

How bind six hoses of assorted sizes
all minus fixtures?
Though his servants shrugged
they dropped to a man on their knees and bound their fingers

tightly around the joints and five small fountains
gushed at specific places
on the lawn
and cooled five straining servants' sweating faces.

Pitiful the little thread of water
that trickle, that distil.
The darkness hid
a general toying with a broken water pistol.

Hid from his daughter, frail organza issue
of his now failing loin
the battle done:
so much militia routed in the man.

Sic transit gloria mundi. I would rather
a different finish.
It was devilish
that the devil denied him that one innocent wish.

TRUCE

My enemy in a purple hat
looks suddenly like a plum
and I am dumb with wonder
at the thought
of feuding with a fruit.

IMAGES OF ANGELS

Imagine them as they were first conceived:
part musical instrument and part daisy
in a white manshape.
Imagine a crowd on the Elysian grass
playing ring-around-a-rosy,
mute except for their singing,
their gold smiles
gold sickle moons in the white sky of their faces.
Sex, neither male nor female,
name and race, in each case, simply angel.

Who, because they are white and gold, has made them holy
but never to be loved or petted, never to be friended?

Not children, who imagine them more simply,
see them more coloured and a deal more cosy,
yet somehow mixed with the father, fearful and fully
realized when the vanishing bed
floats in the darkness,
when the shifting point of focus, that drifting star,
has settled in the head.

More easily perhaps, the little notary
who, given one as a pet, could not
walk the sun-dazzled street
with so lamb-white a companion.
For him its loom-large skeleton—
one less articulated than his own—
would dog his days with doom
until behind the lethal lock
used for his legal documents
he guiltily shut it up.
His terror then that it escape
and smiling call for him at work.
Less dreadful for his public shame
worse for his private guilt
if in the hour that he let it out
he found it limp and boneless as a flower.

Perhaps, more certainly perhaps, the financier.
What business man would buy as he buys stock
as many as could cluster on a pin?
Angels are dropping, angels going up.
He could not mouth such phrases and chagrin
would sugar round his lips as he said 'angel'.
For though he mocks their mention he cannot
tie their tinsel image to a tree
without the momentary lowering of his lids
for fear that they exist in worlds which he
uneasy, reconstructs from childhood's memory.

The archaeologist with his tidy science
had he stumbled upon one unawares,
found as he finds an arrowhead, an angel—
a what-of-a-thing
as primitive as a daisy,
might with his ice cold eye have assessed it coolly.
But how, despite his detailed observations
could he face his learned society and explain?
'Gentlemen, it is thought that they are born
with harps and haloes
as the unicorn with its horn.
Study discloses them white and gold as daisies.'

Perhaps only a dog could accept them wholly,
be happy to follow at their heels
and bark and romp with them in the green fields.

Or, take the nudes of Lawrence and impose
asexuality upon them; those
could meet with ease these gilded albinos.

Or a child, not knowing they were angels could
wander along an avenue hand in hand
with his new milk-white playmates,
take a step

and all the telephone wires would become taut
as the high strings of a harp
and space be merely the spaces between strings
and the world mute, except for a thin singing,
as if a sphere—big enough to be in it
and yet small
so that a glance through the lashes
would show it whole—
were fashioned very finely out of wire
and turning in a wind.

But say the angelic word
and *this* innocent
with his almost-unicorn
would let it go—
(even a child would know
that angels should be flying in the sky!)
and feeling implicated in a lie,
his flesh would grow
cold
and snow
would cover the warm and sunny avenue.

CHIMNEY FIRE

Something must be fire for them, these six
brass-helmeted navy-blue navvies come to chop
the old endlessly-polished wainscot with the fireman's axe.
Ready and royal for crisis and climax
shining and stalwart and valiant—for *this*?
Some element in this puny fire must prove
muscled enough for them to pit against,
and so they invade the green room, all six,
square up to its tidy silence and attack.

Only the roar in the brick and that abating
and the place orderly and quiet as a painting
of a house and all their paraphernalia outside waiting
to be used and useless and inside silence growing coolly
as a lily on a green stem.
Oh how they tackle it, hack it, shout it down
only to find it broken out again,
implacably sending up suckers in the still room,
forevergreen, the chill obverse of flame.

Finally defeat it with their roaring laughter
and helmets on floor and armchair, drinking beer
like an advertisement for a brand name—'after the fire
the dark blue conqueror relaxes here'
in an abandonment of blue and gold
that Rousseau the Douanier might have set
meticulously upon a canvas—those red brick
faces, vacant, those bright axes
and the weltering dark serge angles of arms and legs.

So they attacked their fire and put it out.
No tendril of silence grew in the green room when they went
into the night like night with only the six
stars of their helmets shining omnipotent
in a fiery constellation
pinking the darkness with a sign unknown
to ride the street like a flume, to fan to flame
smouldering branches of artery and vein
in beautiful conflagration, their lovely dream.

BRAZILIAN FAZENDA

That day all the slaves were freed
their manacles, anklets
left on the window ledge to rust in the moist air

and all the coffee ripened
like beads on a bush or balls of fire
as merry as Christmas

and the cows all calved and the calves all lived
such a moo.

On the wide verandah where birds in cages
sang among the bell flowers
I in a bridal hammock
white and tasselled
whistled

and bits fell out of the sky near Nossa Senhora
who had walked all the way in bare feet from Bahia

and the chapel was lit by a child's
fistful of marigolds on the red velvet altar
thrown like a golden ball.

Oh let me come back on a day
when nothing extraordinary happens
so I can stare
at the sugar white pillars
and black lace grills
of this pink house.

BRAZILIAN HOUSE

In this great house white
as a public urinal
I pass my echoing days.
Only the elephant ear leaves
listen outside my window
to the tap of my heels.

Downstairs the laundress
with elephantiasis
sings like an angel
her brown wrists cuffed with suds
and the skinny little black girl
polishing silver laughs to see
her face appear in a tray.

Ricardo, stealthy
lowers his sweating body
into the stream
my car will cross when I
forced by the white porcelain
yammering silence drive
into the hot gold gong
of noon day.

CROSS

He has leaned for hours against the verandah railing
gazing the darkened garden out of mind
while she with battened hatches rides out the wind
that will blow for a year or a day, there is no telling.

As to why they are cross she barely remembers now.
That they *are* cross, she is certain. They hardly speak.
Feel cold and hurt and stony. For a week
have without understanding behaved so.

And will continue so to behave for neither
can come to that undemanded act of love—
kiss the sleeping princess or sleep with the frog—
and break the spell which holds them each from the other.

Or if one ventures towards it, the other, shy
dissembles, regrets too late the dissimulation
and sits hands slack, heart tiny, the hard solution
having again passed by.

Silly the pair of them. Yet they make me weep.
Two on a desert island, back to back
who, while the alien world howls round them black
go their own ways, fall emptily off to sleep.

STORM IN MEXICO

Sky blackening that day over badlands.
Red badlands. Sky blackening, rolling, finally falling.
Rivers of blood cutting wide earth wide open.
Indios out of nowhere in straw raincoats
looking like cornsheaves. Hauling black donkeys.

Our car from another age. Hermetic. Metal.
And rain running on the cornsheaf coats of *los indios*.
Soaking their donkeys. Dissolving their maize plots.
Drumming our hardtop. Our skins dry.
Our hearts uneducated.

ARRAS

Consider a new habit—classical,
and trees espaliered on the wall like candelabra.
How still upon that lawn our sandalled feet.

But a peacock rattling his rattan tail and screaming
has found a point of entry. Through whose eye
did it insinuate in furled disguise
to shake its jewels and silk upon that grass?

The peaches hang like lanterns. No one joins
those figures on the arras.
                                    Who am I
or who am I become that walking here
I am observer, other, Gemini,
starred for a green garden of cinema?

I ask, what did they deal me in this pack?
The cards, all suits, are royal when I look.
My fingers slipping on a monarch's face
twitch and grow slack.
I want a hand to clutch, a heart to crack.

No one is moving now, the stillness is
infinite. If I should make a break . . .
take to my springy heels . . . ? But nothing moves.
The spinning world is stuck upon its poles,
the stillness points a bone at me. I fear
the future on this arras.
                                    I confess:

It was my eye.

Voluptuous it came.
Its head the ferrule and its lovely tail
folded so sweetly; it was strangely slim
to fit the retina. And then it shook
and was a peacock—living patina,
eye-bright, maculate!
Does no one care?

I thought their hands might hold me if I spoke.
I dreamed the bite of fingers in my flesh,
their poke smashed by an image, but they stand
as if within a treacle, motionless,
folding slow eyes on nothing.
                    While they stare
another line has trolled the encircling air,
another bird assumes its furled disguise.

TRAVELLERS' PALM

Miraculously plaited tree.
A sailor's knot
rooted,
a growing fan
whose grooved and slanted branches
are aqueducts
end-stopped
for tropical rains.

Knot, fan,
Quixote's windmill,
what-you-will—
for me, traveller,
a well.

On a hot day I took
a sharp and pointed knife,
plunged,
and water gushed
to my cupped mouth

old water
tasting green,
of vegetation and dust,
old water, warm as tears.

And in that tasting,
taster, water, air,
in temperature identical
were so
intricately merged
a fabulous foreign bird
flew silent from a void

lodged in my boughs.

In the Wake (detail)

The Dance (detail)

The Red Garden (detail)

Labyrinth

CRY ARARAT!

I

In the dream the mountain near
but without sound.
A dream through binoculars
seen sharp and clear:
the leaves moving, turning
in a far wind
no ear can hear.

First soft in the distance,
blue in blue air
then sharpening, quickening
taking on green.
Swiftly the fingers
seek accurate focus
(the bird
has vanished so often
before the sharp lens
could deliver it)
then as if from the sea
the mountain appears
emerging new-washed
growing maples and firs.
The faraway, here.

Do not reach to touch it
nor labour to hear.
Return to your hand
the sense of the hand;
return to your ear
the sense of the ear.
Remember the statue,
that space in the air
which with nothing to hold
what the minute is giving
is through each point
where its marble touches air.

Then will each leaf and flower
each bird and animal
become as perfect as
the thing its name evoked
when busy as a child
the world stopped at the Word
and Flowers more real than flowers
grew vivid and immense;
and Birds more beautiful
and Leaves more intricate
flew, blew and quilted all
the quick landscape.

So flies and blows the dream
embracing like a sea
all that in it swims
when dreaming, you desire
and ask for nothing more
than stillness to receive
the I-am animal,
the We-are leaf and flower,
the distant mountain near.

II

So flies and blows the dream that haunts us when we wake
to the unreality of bright day:
the far thing almost sensed by the still skin
and then the focus lost, the mountain gone.
This is the loss that haunts our daylight hours
leaving us parched at nightfall
blowing like last year's leaves
sibilant on blossoming trees
and thirsty for the dream of the mountain
more real than any event:
more real than strangers passing on the street
in a city's architecture white as bone
or the immediate companion.

But sometimes there is one
raw with the dream of flying:
'I, a bird,
landed that very instant
and complete—
as if I had drawn a circle in my flight
and filled its shape—
find air a perfect fit.
But this my grief,
that with the next tentative lift
of my indescribable wings
the ceiling looms
heavy as a tomb.

'Must my most exquisite and private dream
remain unleavened?
Must this flipped and spinning coin that sun
could gild and make miraculous become
so swiftly pitiful?
The vision of the flight it imitates
burns brightly in my head as if a star
rushed down to touch me where I stub against
what must forever be my underground.'

III

These are the dreams that haunt us,
these the fears.
Will the grey weather wake us,
toss us twice in the terrible night to tell us
the flight is cancelled
and the mountain lost?

O, then cry Ararat!

The dove believed
in her sweet wings and in the rising peak
with such a washed and easy innocence
that she found rest on land for the sole of her foot
and, silver, circled back,
a green twig in her beak.

The leaves that make the tree by day,
the green twig the dove saw fit
to lift across a world of water
break in a wave about our feet.
The bird in the thicket with his whistle
the crystal lizard in the grass
the star and shell
tassel and bell
of wild flowers blowing where we pass,
this flora-fauna flotsam, pick and touch,
requires the focus of the total I.

A single leaf can block a mountainside;
all Ararat be conjured by a leaf.

PREPARATION

Go out of your mind.
Prepare to go mad.
Prepare to break
split along cracks
inhabit the darks of your eyes
inhabit the whites.

Prepare to be huge.
Be prepared to be small
the least molecule of
an unlimited form.
Be a limited form
and spin in your skin
one point in its whole.

Be prepared to prepare
for what you have dreamed
to burn and be burned
to burst like a pod
to break at your seams.

Be pre-pared. And pre-pare.
But it's never like that.
It is where you are not
that the fissure occurs
and the light crashes in.

THE FILLED PEN

Eager to draw again,
find space in that small room
for my drawing-board and inks
and the huge revolving world
the delicate nib releases.

I have only to fill my pen
and the shifting gears begin:
fly-wheel and cog-wheel start
their small-toothed interlock

and whatever machinery draws
is drawing through my fingers
and the shapes that I have drawn
gaze up into my eyes.
We stare each other down.

Light of late afternoon—
white wine across my paper—
the subject I would draw.
Light of the stars and sun.

Light of the swan-white moon.
The blazing light of trees.
And the rarely glimpsed bright face
behind the apparency of things.

THREE GOLD FISH

I feel quite sure those three gold fish I saw
burning like Blake's *Tyger* in the pool
were real all right.
The pool was different too.
It seemed to swell
like some great crystalline and prismed tear
and brim and never spill
and those fish burned within it
burned and shone
and left their brand—
a piscine fleur-de-lys—
stamped on the air, on me,
on skin and hair
spinning to giddy heaven.

Sharp and clear
that fiery image burns within me still:
those three gold fish
the pool
the altered air
and I—observing and observed—
a high
point on a twirling spindle which
spun and hurled great gilded lariats.

FOR MSTISLAV ROSTROPOVICH WITH LOVE

Listening ear
a conduit for these sounds,
I watch your bowing arm
and see beneath
your sleeve, shirtcuff
and pliant sheath of skin,
a wrist of stainless steel
precision-turned,
fluid with bearings,
bright as adamant
with power to blind us
like a silver sun;
while gazing fearless
fire into fire
the enduring pupil
of my inner eye
made in the manner
that you made your wrist—
of matter primal and alchemical
impervious to accident
or hurt.

This is already much.
But there is more:
what falls apart is held together
each
atom aligned
and in its proper place.
So great an order interlocks my flesh
that I, as centred
as a spinning top
am perfectly asleep
(which, in this sense
means, if not *perfectly*
then *more* awake).

And as an atom—
one among these rapt
like-centred listeners—
I am part
of that essential
intricate design
which forms a larger unit—
mutable
around its sleeping core—
while it, in turn,
part of a vaster
one I barely glimpse—
already cosmic—
leads us to the stars.

Maestro, *salud.*
Perfection in an art
can heal an open wound,
a broken heart
or fuse fragmented man.

Tonight, are we not proof?

AFTER READING *ALBINO PHEASANTS*

For Pat Lane

Pale beak . . . pale eye . . . the dark imagination
flares like magnesium. Add but *pale flesh*
and I am lifted to a weightless world:
watered cerulean, chrome-yellow (light)
and green, veronese—if I remember—a soft wash
recalls a summer evening sky.

At Barro de Navidad we watched the sky
fade softly like a bruise. Was it imagination
that showed us Venus phosphorescent in a wash
of air and ozone?—a phosphorescence flesh
wears like a mantle in bright moonlight,
a natural skin-tone in that other world.

Why should I wish to escape this world?
Why should three phrases alter the colour of the sky
the clarity, texture even, of the light?
What is there about the irrepressible imagination
that the adjective *pale* modifying *beak, eye* and *flesh*
can set my sensibilities awash?

If with my thickest brush I were to lay a wash
of thinnest watercolour I could make a world
as unlike my own dense flesh
as the high-noon midsummer sky;
but it would not catch at my imagination
or change the waves or particles of light

yet *pale* can tip the scales, make light
this heavy planet. If I were to wash
everything I own in mercury, would imagination
run rampant in that suddenly silver world—
free me from gravity, set me floating sky-
ward—thistledown—permanently disburdened of my flesh?

Like cygnets hatched by ducks, our minds and flesh
are imprinted early—what to me is light
may be dark to one born under a sunny sky.
And however cool the water my truth won't wash
without shrinking except in its own world
which is one part matter, nine parts imagination.

I fear flesh which blocks imagination,
the light of reason which constricts the world.
Pale beak . . . pale eye . . . pale flesh . . . My sky's awash.

STAR-GAZER

The very stars are justified.
The galaxy
italicized.

I have proof-read
and proof-read
the beautiful script.

There are no
errors.

LEATHER JACKET

One day the King laid hold on one of
the peacocks and gave orders that he should
be sewn up in a leather jacket.—SUHRAWARDI

That peacock a prisoner
that many-eyed bird
blind.

Enclosed in a huge leather purse.
Locked in darkness.
All its pupils sealed
its tiny brain sealed
its light and fluttering heart
heavy as a plum.

Its life vegetable.
That beautiful colourful bird
a root vegetable.

Cry, cry for the peacock
hidden in heavy leather
sewn up in heavy leather
in the garden

among flowers
and flowering trees
near streams
and flowering fountains
among cicadas
and singing birds.

The peacock sees nothing
smells nothing
hears nothing at all
remembers nothing

but a terrible yearning
a hurt beyond bearing
an almost memory
of a fan of feathers
a growing garden

and sunshine falling
as light as pollen.

THE DISGUISES

You, my Lord, were dressed in astonishing disguises:
as a Chinese Emperor, ten feet tall,
as a milk-skinned woman
parading in exquisite stuffs.

You were ambiguous and secret
and hidden in other faces.

How did we know you were there at all?
Your ineffable presence
perfumed the air like an avenue of lilacs.

AFTER DONNE

A door whines and I go. Or a fly drones
and reactive, I almost buzz.
Am subject to every tic and toc.
Ears' energy frenetic.
Likewise eyes'.
Distractable.
Unexpected red, green, blue
signal and I respond.

For the least moving speck
I neglect God and all his angels
yet attention's funnel—
a macaw's eye—contracts,
becomes a vortex.

I have been sucked through.

FLY: ON WEBS

Two kinds of web: the one
not there. A sheet of glass.
Look! I am flying through air,
spinning in emptiness . . . SPUNG!
. . . bounced on a flexible wire,
caught by invisible guys.

The other a filigree, gold
as the call of a trumpet. A sun
to my myriad-faceted eye.
A season. A climate. Compelled
and singing hosannas I fly:
I dazzle. I struggle. I drown.

SHAMAN

Now to be healed of an old wound requires
diet, cautery, exercise and spells.

The shaman is solemn.
He burns herbs.
The air is moiréed, rainbowed even.
I am chilled.
In the folds of his intricate robes
of feathers, furs
beads like a bird's eyes
pale polished bone,
his curled hands lie
one upon the other, relaxed, as if asleep.
Hands curiously painted with my name and yours.

Messages are transmitted mind to mind.
For just as long as he wishes
my mind twins his.
Small images of you form and fill my head.
They are leaden images and heavy as lead.
Weigh down my eyelids
weigh down my head
torso, arms, legs, feet.
I am a dead weight held fast to the dead.
White wires pin and bind me.
Am I asleep?

He prescribes salves and potions, uses words
from another language.
The lines of his face spell out undecipherable messages.
When he opens his lips to speak he displays a jade
green satiny lining to his mouth and throat.
Is he *Diphyllodes magnificus* in disguise?
Tropical? Pied plumage of paradise?
I am no longer certain.
Is he man? Or bird?

It is all that twittering perhaps.
Short vowels. Long.
Quick clicking consonants.
Inscrutable eyes
bright as black currants.
Tall curious plumes
nodding as he moves.
Faint peppery whiff of dung.

Ancient nomadic snowman has rolled round.
His spoor: a wide swathe on the white ground
signs of a wintry struggle where he stands.

Stands? Yes, he stands. What snowman sat?
Legless, indeed, but more as if he had
legs than had not.

White double O, white nothing nothing, this
the child's first man on a white paper, his
earliest and fistful image is

now three-dimensional. Abstract. Everyman.
Of almost manna, he is still no man
no person, this so personal snowman.

O transient un-inhabitant, I know
no child who, on seeing the leprous thaw
undo your whitened torso and face of snow

would not, had he the magic
call you back
from that invisible attack

even knowing he can, with the new miracle
of another and softer and whiter snowfall
make you again, this time more wonderful.

SNOWMAN

Innocent single snowman. Overnight
brings him—a bright
omen—a thunderbolt of white.

But once I saw a mute in every yard
come like a plague; a stock-still multitude
and all stone-buttoned, bun-faced and absurd.

And next day they were still there but each
had changed a little as if all had inched
forward or back, I barely knew which;

and greyed a little too, grown sinister
and disreputable in their sooty fur,
numb, unmoving and nothing moving near.

And as far as I could see the snow was scarred
only with angels' wing marks or the feet of birds
like twigs broken upon the snow or shards

discarded. And I could hear no sound
as far as I could hear except a round
kind of an echo without end

rung like a hoop below them and above
jarring the air they had no need of
in a landscape without love.

CHINESE BOXES

Box within box.
I know the order, know
large to small diminishing until
that cube the size of sugar—like a die—
is cast within its core
and therein set—dimensionless—
an all-ways turning eye—
a dot, an aleph, which
with one swift glance
sees heaven and hell united
as a globe
in whose harmonious spinning
day and night
and birth and death are conjured into one,
where seasons lie like compass points
and where, twinned with its answer,
question is born null.

Box within box.
From small to large increasing—
angles, blocks,
enormous, made of plexiglass,
the sky
filling with them,
visible as air
is visible when briefly smoked with breath
until their structures grow too large and sheer
for sight to encompass—
cellophane box kites
huge as the Kaaba
luminous as ice
and imperceptible to any sense
more coarse than sightings of that inner eye
which sees the absolute
in emptiness.

FULL MOON

I search all cupboards for my lunar topee
and find its crescent-shaped
bull's horns
glimmering phosphorus among my hats—
a minotaur among domestic sheep.

Pale female Viking venturing into night,
I dare the full moon's innocent vague stare
in Mother Goddess guise
while left and right
my sober neighbours beat their wives and rave.

DOT

Hurl your giant thunderbolt that on my heart
falls gently as a feather, falls and fills
each crease and cranny of me—a chinook:
sweet water, head to foot.

With lightning stagger me so I may stand
centred as never otherwise. In stock-
stillness, dizzying movement find.
Spinning, a dot.

All-of-a-piece, seamless; with the warp and woof
afterwards/before. The stuff spun
without stop or selvedge—measureless
continuum.

Visible/invisible. Golden. Clear
as any crystal. How to name it? How
to loose or hold—for held is holder here
and holder held.

Harry me. Hurry me to spaces where
my Father's house has many dimensions.
Tissue of tesseract.
A sphered sphere.

THE YELLOW PEOPLE IN
METAMORPHOSIS

Lunar Phase

Not only silvered
One dimension less

Moon's light
falls thin and flat

on metal shapes
that heave and strive

immobile
but alive

Earthly Phase

i

In topazes and amber
mango, peach
the yellow people hive
the yellow people swarm
just beyond our hearing
just beyond our sight
Their chromosomes
and yellow genes
squeezed from a tube
of cadmium
their canary-coloured
hair and skin
and eyes
are palest
cadmium

Molecular
they stretch and grow
Don waggish wigs
wear caps, capes, cloaks
gamboge and chrome

Crave mosaics
small moorish patterns
checks   greek key
all intricate shapes
fine mottle   stipple
singing reeds
whistles of birds

Whose notes are these?
That trill? Did (s)he
flicker a yellow throat muscle?
Do wiry yellow curls vibrate?
A springed instrument? Is s(he)
crossed with a flute?
That crown
a splendid yellow bony comb
grown from the cranium

The yellow people hive
the yellow people swarm
just beyond our hearing
just beyond belief

Warblers in the leaves?
Peaches in the trees?
An antic
trick
of light?

ii

Stamp   Stamp   I feel them weighty
Wonderful acrobats clanking about
loud in the next dimension
luring my inner eye
and growing huge and yellow
Ballooning gunny-sacks
striving to sunhood
not yet sunny
rayed
as dandelions

and lighter far
than their looming size suggests
See them throw ballast up to another ether
Ascend
hand over fist

Yet one least glance aside
shows me their scale of gold
ladders that come and go
They alter as they climb
and shining chains and cones
reach down to draw them up
as known to unknown spanned
with weightless veins and bones
transforming all their yellow
they golden   glow
and
      vanish

iii

An orison of them stars my farthest heaven

Vertical
these almost alchemists
gilders of nimbi
leaf the chieftain's feathers
sol's flames   cock's crest
bright leo's sunburst locks

Make sovereign all my pocketful of copper

Solar Phase

This is another matter
Seventh heaven
Among celestial celandines to eat
one apple for eternity

(I know
nothing of what I speak
I speak
nothing of what I know)

ANOTHER SPACE

Those people in a circle on the sand
are dark against its gold
turn like a wheel
revolving in a horizontal plane
whose axis—do I dream it?—
vertical
invisible
immeasurably tall
rotates a starry spool.

Yet *if* I dream
why in the name of heaven are fixed parts
within me set in motion
like a poem?

Those people in a circle reel me in.
Down the whole length of golden beach I come
willingly pulled by their rotation
slow
as a moon pulls waters
on a string
their turning circle winds around its rim.

I see them there in three dimensions yet
their height implies another space
their clothes'
surprising chiaroscuro postulates
a different spectrum.
What kaleidoscope
does air construct
that all their movements make a compass rose
surging and altering?
I speculate
on some dimension I can barely guess.

Nearer I see them dark-skinned.
They are dark. And beautiful.
Great human sunflowers spinning in a ring
cosmic as any bumble-top
the vast
procession of the planets in their dance.
And nearer still I see them—'a Chagall'—
each fiddling on an instrument—its strings
of some black woollen fibre
and its bow—feathered—
an arrow almost.
Arrow is.

For now the headman—one step forward—shoots
(or does he bow or does he lift a kite
up and over the bright pale dunes of air?)
to strike the absolute centre of my skull
my absolute centre somehow
with such skill
such staggering lightness
that the blow is love.

And something in me melts.
It is as if a glass partition melts—
or something I had always thought was glass—
some pane that halved my heart
is proved, in its melting, ice.

And to-fro all the atoms pass
in bright osmosis
hitherto
in stasis locked
where now a new
direction opens like an eye.

SNOWSHOES

Flat   twin
lacrosse sticks
laced
with oil-lamp wicks

Two eyes
of Horus
one above the other

I smell wet moccasins
see beads on fire

What a beautiful lattice:
babiche: pale strips
of wolf gut
stretched
on wooden frames
Red bobbles
on far toe-tips

It is 20 below

The air burning

Fingers are thick and slow
Lumps of lead
at the ends of my legs
move rattan pontoons
through a smoke of snow

I climb a drift
hear it pack
and hold
sky-high on the prairie

This engineering—
the reverse of wings—
is achieved from below

How is it on water?

The question
never
quite beyond earshot
comes wagging   comes wagging

LEVIATHAN IN A POOL

. . . It was a small whale, a Porpoise about eight feet long
with lovely subtle curves glistening in the cold rain. It had
been mutilated. Someone had hacked off its flukes for a
souvenir. Two other people had carved their initials deeply
into its side, and someone else had stuck a cigar butt in its
blowhole. I removed the cigar and stood there a long time
with feelings I cannot describe. —ROGER S. PAYNE

Leviathan in a Pool

I

Black and white plastic
inflatable
a child's giant toy
teeth perfectly conical
tongue pink
eyes where ears are
blowhole (fontanelle
a rip in a wet inner tube
Third Eye)
out of which speech
breath
and beautiful fountains flower

So much for linear description
phrases in place of whale

This creature fills that pool
as an eye its socket
Moves   laughs like an eye
shines like an eye   eyebright
eyeshaped   mandorla
of meeting worlds
forked tail attached
and fin
like a funny sail

It is rotund and yet
flexible as a whip
Lighter than air going up
and heavy as a truckload of bricks
It leaps sky-high   it flies
and comes down *whack*
on its freshly painted side
and the spectators get wet
drenched
soaked to the hide

Tongue lolling like a dog's
after a fast run
pleased with itself   and you
it seems to want to be petted
rears its great head up
hangs it   its tiny eyes gleam
Herring   minute as whitebait
slip down its throat
Dear whale we say as if to a child
We beam

And it disappears   Utterly
with so dark a thrust
of its muscle
through silver tines
of water
only streamers of brine
tiny tinsels of brine
remain

II

Swim round the pool vocalizing   the boy says
and *Toot* they call through their blowholes
Toot toot   Toot
At sea they will sometimes sing for thirty minutes
cadences   recognizable series of notes   songs which carry
hundreds of miles   Sing together   Sing singly

Here in a small pool they vocalize on command
joyous short toots   calls

Why am I crying?

III

Haida and Nootka respond to whistle signals
Each whistle has its own pitch
and each whale knows which is which

Haida and Nootka respond to hand signals
Fresh from the wild Pacific
they answer to hand signals

(The words are for us
who have not yet learned
that two blasts
mean

Give your trainer a big kiss
or a flick of the wrist
means   *Vocalize*)

Chimo   white as Moby
albino and still a baby
is deaf
and has poor vision
like white cats

(white men and women?)

so Chimo
cannot respond to hand or whistle

Yet this high-spirited
'lissom'
girl of a whale
unexpectedly pale

as if caught undressed
performs
She leaps like Nootka
flaps like Haida
vocalizes

What are her cues and signals?
In what realm
do her lightning actions rise?

I lean upon the pool's wet rail
Through eyes'
sightless sideways glances
seem to see
a red line on the air
as bright as blood
that threads them on one string
trainer and whales

Visitor

Look whale
earthbound airbound me
eager visitor
constant true
at your tankside

I'm the one
indistinguishable from
all your other aging fans:
inert bespectacled opaque

Where I differ
if I do
I can kick the chandelier
turn a cartwheel on the lawn

I break my barriers where I can
Challenge gravity as do you

Nootka Chimo Haida

I

Precocious   Aggressive   Skinny
Nootka took
the pool in her breach
It was hers   And Haida too
Her male
She grabbed at tourists
where they touched the rail
Was starved   Libidinous
Ate
a hundredweight

When Haida failed to
display for her
she fought
a black and white whale on fire
and flashing red
in a frenzy of skills and rages
Haida hid
Chimo developed a skin disease
lost weight

Nootka must go
Not home   Not back to sea
to its tangle of weeds
its shoals   its schools of bright
little fishes blown from glass
but swung
by crane and sling
to a waiting truck

What giant fishmonger
laid her body out
on that bed of ice?
What monstrous nurse
smeared vaseline round her blowhole

and on the bare
and drying continents of her skin?
What practised parceller
wrapped her tonnage up
in a long wet wind of sheets
so she rode the blistering air
a blimp in shrouds
lumbering down the highway
along the green
peninsula
to the winged machine?

It took tackle and hoist
to heave her up to the plane
Two fiery hours to angle her body through
the inadequate door
Four hours from the time
they had hauled her out of her pen
she was all aboard   and blind
cigar in a tube
but quick   live blubber and bone
Incredible bird

And in those four hours
'she flailed about only once'
and high and small
as a flying gull
'cried only occasionally'

II

NOVEMBER SECOND NINETEEN SEVENTY-TWO

CHIMO DEAD
OF CHEDIAK-HIGASHI SYNDROME
FOUND IN THE MORNING DEAD
BELLY UP IN THE POOL
WHITE GOLDFISH IN A BOWL

BELLY UP IN THE POOL
FOUND IN THE MORNING DEAD
OF CHEDIAK-HIGASHI SYNDROME
CHIMO DEAD

NOVEMBER SECOND NINETEEN SEVENTY-TWO

III

We still don't know how much of Haida's
problem is physical and how much emotional.

Thunderbolt shot
he lolls about

Refuses food
Is forcibly fed

giant egg-nogs
mega-vitamins   drugs

We all partake
of his heartbreak

Who can console
a bereaved whale?

Boy with a flute
plays a sweet note

Haida responds
with such sad sounds

What will restore
his lost ardor?

O wise men who look
in treatise and book

for remedy
had you thought of the sea?

THEY MIGHT HAVE BEEN ZEBRAS

For Margaret

They might have been zebras. I'd have been no more surprised
than to see by daylight four night raccoons, full-grown
walking bear-like in indian file across
our isthmus of bright grass
so black and white, their fur so fluffed and upright
black masked, tails ringed with black and white
utterly foreign to morning's minted light
and violent as newsprint on the viridian lawn.

It's not that they're unfamiliar. We have met
dozens of times in darkness. They've climbed and gazed
down at me from the Douglas fir's right-angled boughs—
sly and furtive watchers—or, bold and wild
hauled from our obsidian pool gold fish whose scales
in the moonlight shine like pieces of eight.
We acknowledge each other at night. We meet and stare
shadowy form at shadowy form. I chain the dog
leave offerings for them of marshmallows, raisins, bread.

But by day they immobilize me. I hold my breath.
Turn to a great soft statue with inflammable eyes
tinder for the fire they strike from the morning air.
And I see them blacker and whiter than I had dreamed
sharper, more feral, spanning the grassy isthmus
as if there might be others in front and behind—
a whole parade extending to both horizons
but hidden by the berried cotoneasters.

When they disappear I am released.
Dart through the door.
The sun is sharpening every leaf.
Its threads are spinning a golden tent.
The green is enamel or emeralds.
Petals fall more fragile than flakes of snow.
I alone, unbeautiful, in the whole morning
in flapping nightdress search every bush.
But the four who blinded me are gone.
Is this grey ash all that is left?

A BACKWARDS JOURNEY

When I was a child of say, seven
I still had serious attention to give
to everyday objects. The Dutch Cleanser—
which was the kind my mother bought—
in those days came in a round container
of yellow cardboard around which ran
the very busy Dutch Cleanser woman
her face hidden behind her bonnet
holding a yellow Dutch Cleanser can
on which a smaller Dutch Cleanser woman
was holding a smaller Dutch Cleanser can
on which a minute Dutch Cleanser woman
held an imagined Dutch Cleanser can . . .

This was no game. The woman led me
backwards through the eye of the mind
until she was the smallest point
my thought could hold to. And at that moment
I think I knew that if no one called
and nothing broke the delicate jet
of my attention, that tiny image
could smash the atom of space and time.

THE MAZE

I clearly recall the feel of the clipped hedges—
laurel or box—I am not sure which.
I was still small
so the little leaves of box
would have seemed bigger.
I remember they shone, looked black in places, scratched
the skin of my wrists and ankles as I passed.

Overhead the sky was light,
a faint cirrus,
duck-egg changing to golden like a wing,
but the shadow cast by the hedge
threw a chill upon me
as I kept to the curve that drew me in
and in.
Compelled, and carrying out a strange instruction—
vital, timeless, tangible as a thread—
I was tracing the spiral nebula in my head.

When I think of it now I remember the path frozen
and how, on the inside edge of a bowed skate,
I arrived at the heart of the maze in a clean sweep,
reached 'le Ciel' in a long unbroken spiral.

Yet the truth of the matter escapes.
There is no returning
beyond the sudden narrowing of the curve—
(eye of the nautilus, the ram's horn).
Memory fails me at every try.
I follow
the spiralling pathway over and over, run—
hoping to pass that place on the sharpening turn—
to grow small, then smaller, smaller still—and enter
the maze's vanishing point, a spark, extinguished.

CULLEN REVISITED

Cullen at fifty, arsonist, set fire
to the whole accumulation. Rings, wrongs, rights
from buds of flame burst into flower,
burned like magnesium—white—or red as rags.
The bag of tricks banged off—flared, fumed, smoked.
Butt ends of jokes, lexicons, old chains like briars
glowed in the night sky. Strange constellations rose.
The conflagration could be seen for miles.

Cullen among the charred remains—himself
down to the bone—scuffed, shuffled, poked.
Recognized nothing. The span of his life reduced
to nails, pearl buttons, gravel, twists of wire—
all hard, all black, all useless. Cullen smiled
and a wind arose like the wind the Holy Ghost
bears in its wings—and the flames broke out and smoked
and flickered in white and gold before they died
for the second time in a feathery ash as grey
and soft as feathers plucked from a dove.

Cullen, departing, stubbed his toe, upturned
(darkened face of the moon at solar eclipse)
a disc, heart-sized and heavy for its size.
Makeweight, touchstone, lodestar. And this he kept.
It squinted where he rubbed it.
Like an eye.

So Cullen began again. Trees bloomed. Sun shone.
And he, the Ace of Wands, green-sprigged, was borne
high in a Giant Hand through a running sky.
At night in a rain of shooting stars, he slept.
The heart as a Rose, Imperial palms—and jewels
from an underground cavern filled his head.

Veins on fire, he dreamed the grey days through
like a wintering bear. He waked
to tea-coloured kings and queens upright as staves—
small, wren-boned, walking in purple, heads
bound in embroideries, braceleted wrists—
and all reflected as though in water, twinned
like royalty in a card deck.
                              Cullen slept
and tall, black naked warriors like divs
sprang from the earth like grain—green at the groin—
constructed walls of intricate mosaics,
each stone polished and cut and then exactly placed.
As Cullen waked, the sly disc winked and shone.

All this was in World One.
                              World Two was where
he explored the golden ship—cabins and hold—
hoisted its golden sails and from its gold
crow's nest sighted—Third World . . .
hazy at first, and seen from his position,
half-way between earth and heaven,
half-blinded by the sun,
seeming to rock.
                  And hum.

MELANIE'S NITE-BOOK

Note

I am not Melanie.
We do not know one another.
Yet her poems found among my papers paint
the underside of something I have known—
a parallel existence in a key
significantly lower.

They have their place
strike their own note, distort, darken
the belling
light.

Mother

She said I gave her her jewelled breasts
and he, my father, her jewelled pubis
In return, she gave me a diamond heart
a splinter of ice for either eye

In this family potlatch I want no part
I am giving her back her diamond heart

Sister

Sister little idiot one
whom I loved
and who loved me
like a plant perhaps
or bird
tamed by kindness
set apart
from another planet
where
other laws prevail
and who
barely entered
in this race

part of me
o part of me

Father

Father, o farther
in what heaven circl'st thou?
Daily and dearly
ask I for thy succor

I see thee now
the red crease on thy brow
left where thy cap had rested
Crested ring
Buttons of brightest brass
High boots' high shine
dusty with pollen

from the flowering grass
of that unrolling upland
whose sweet air
was black and white
with magpies' flight
rank sweat of thy black horse

Father, o farther
forc'st thou me to range
world-wide world over
searching evermore
obedient, house-trained
heel-trained, at thy call?

Who sett'st the world on fire
for others quenched
my smallest fire
uncoiled its acrid smoke
Whose flute thou lettest
others hear, whose drum . . .
My silence only
golden in thine ear

Father, o father
trembl'st thou with dread
of my grey gaze
the twin of thy grey gaze?
I small, large-eyed
crunched in a tiny space
awaiting thy benediction
thy hand upon my head

Father, o father
cravest thou my grace?
Cravest forgiveness
for thy just rebukes
as I still crave thy praise

striving for thy approval
to appear
beautiful in thine eyes
or talented?

Father, Father
can we call a truce?
Our binary stardom cancel
you from me
set free after how long—
two lifetimes? three?—
by that one word
which severs as it heals

Let me your spokesman
and your axeman be

Brother

You wore the looks I longed for
almond eyes
black from our gypsy forebears
milky skin
The creamy manner of your expensive school
lay sleek upon you
I was thin
acneyed and angular
No 'pretty girl'

Dreamed you displayed me
like a football trophy
took me to stag rock sessions
hockey games
places where I could loose
my female trace
my faint unearthly scent
my moon-pale face
Your slim twin sister
beautiful as Euclid

For it was written
All the ordered atoms
in orderly heaven
had ordained it so
And we obeyed that order
like a team
of harnessed horses driven
by skilled compassionate hands
or as a pair
of eagles riding
transparent muscles of air

Wakened to your abuse
the pale grey mornings
broke day after day
littered my room
your inkblots
on my notebooks
my stamps missing
no honey in the comb

Invented heroes to protect
young men
with fatal wounds
or dark congenital scars
White-meat invisible princes
sapphire-eyed
crippled
tubercular
Incurable invalids
who found me sweet as myrrh

These my companions
as I rode the subway
or climbed the interminable
steps to school
my co-conspirators
who let me love them
whom I called 'brother'
all my sister years

Ancestors

The cavernous theatre filled with them,
going back
generation on generation,
dressed in the colours of power:
scarlet and purple and black,
plumed and surpliced and gowned.
Men with arrogant Roman faces,
women like thoroughbred horses
held in check.

These were the people for whom
I had lived in exemplary fashion,
had not let down,
for whom I'd refrained from evil,
borne pain with grace.
And now they were here—resurrected—
the damned demanding dead,
jamming a theatre like head-cheese,
smelling of moth-balls and scent,
brilliantine, shoe-polish, brasso
and old brocade.

Row after row
and tier after tier they ranged,
crowded together like eels
in the orchestra pit,
squeezed in the quilted boxes
and blocking the aisles
while I, on the stage alone,
last of the line,
pinned by the nails of their eyes,
was expected to give an account.

But the gypsies came in the nick
and flung themselves about.
They stamped their naked feet
dark with the dust of Spain,
clattered their castanets,
rattled their tambourines,
brandished their flashing knives
and put the lot to rout.

The Child

I dreamed the child was dead
and folded in a box
like stockings or a dress.

I dreamed its toys and games
its brightly coloured clothes
were lying on the grass

and with them I was left
adult and dutiful
with ink instead of blood.

I could not bear the grief
accommodate the loss—
as if my heart had died.

On wakening I saw
the child beside my bed
Not dead! not dead! I cried.

But startled by my voice
and fearful of my glance
the phantom infant fled.

What little the birds had overlooked
I found—
a first few meagre crumbs that led me on
from dark to darkest,
then the trail grew clear,
for deep in the airless wood
not even birds
ventured,
not enough sun,
no space to spread
their impeccable feathered arms.
(My wings were plucked.
Pin-feathers here and there.)

Whatever small rodents overlooked
I ate.
A skimpy nourishment.
It hurt my eyes
this meticulous search for food.
I might have stopped—
'stoppered', the word I want,
comparative,
a bottle sealed
inert, inanimate,
unable to move or open of itself.
(*I* could not move.
It moved me, opened me.)

Whatever they dropped for me
was miraculous,
multiple-purpose—food and way in one,
wakening me from nightmare,
leading on
out of that shadowy landscape
into dawn.

Rose of the air unfolding,
petal and thorn.
(A pencil sketch
with pale transparent wash—
watercolour on rice paper,
a wide brush.)
And sun, up with a rush.

The world gold-leafed and burnished:
gilded trees,
leaves like a jeweller's handwork,
grasses, ferns
filigreed and enamelled—Byzantine.
Cresses in clusters, bunched
beside a stream—
a glittering gold chain,
gold mesh, gold sheen,
where I bent down to drink.
(What birds then sang?)
Gold water in my mouth,
gold of my dreams
slipping like sovereigns
through my gold-rinsed hands.

THE FIRST PART

Great desire to write it all.
Is it age, death's heavy breath
making absolute autobiography
urgent?

Who would think that this old hive
housed such honey?
Could one guess
blue and gold of a macaw
blue and gold of sky and sun
could set up such melodic din
beat so musical a drum?

Distilled from all this living,
all this gold.

1. To begin before I was born.
    Little Joy riding a cloud
    saw it all, merely smiled—
    this planet's snares, seducers, tears—
    knew it all. Simply smiled.

2. Man in black.
    Raggedy jacket, shiny pants.
    Victim of St Vitus' Dance.
    Animated scarecrow made of bones,
    jerking, tweaking down the street.
    Strings tangled.
    Nerves jangled.

            My small pink coat
            my scarlet shoes
            drained of colour,
            somehow . . . broke.

3. They removed her golden wig.
    Underneath, as if trepanned,
    her head was like a china cup.
    Eyes that could no longer shut
    were taken out.

Re-aligned, the leaden weight.
Glassy eyes in pairs on hooks
stared in dozens from the walls.

That visit finished me for dolls.

4.   A woman with wet palms who took my hand.

I prayed the Lord my palms be wet.

5.   Lost ring. Lost ring.
She lost it. Lost it.
Pain
of that loss
lay on us
summerlong.
And then to my bright eye
the gleam in the grass.
The gold in the green
beneath the snow-apple tree.

I glimpsed the changed
geometry of Eden.
Transparent bird
in its transparent shell.

6.   White quartz
red-veined,
cerulean-veined
and jade,
found in the crawl-space
under the verandah
with grown-ups walking
talking overhead.

My secret garden.
Magic. Mineral.

7. Horse. High as a house. Smooth as a nut.
   Its flaring nostrils snorted dragon's breath
   or snuffled, tickling. Its velvet lips
   lifted the accurate white sugar lump
   exactly from my flat extended palm.
   And crunch. The curving yellowish ivory teeth.

8. Agates and alleys. Smokies. Glassies.
   Tumbling galaxies of them. Worlds.
   A dark disappearing one which whirled
   and a spiral one which drew me in
   to vanishing point at its poles.

9. Backdrop: the cordillera of the Rockies.
   Infinity—slowly spinning in the air—
   invisibly entered through the holes of gophers,
   visibly, in a wigwam's amethyst smoke.

   Eternity implicit on the prairie.
   One's self the centre of a boundless dome
   so balanced in its horizontal plane
   and sensitively tuned that one's least move
   could fractionally tip it North, South, East.

   Westward, in undulations of beige turf,
   the fugal foothills changed their rhythm, rose
   to break in fire and snow. My Hindu Khush.

   > It was a landscape in which things could grow
   > enormous. Full of struts. A prairie sky
   > builds an immense meccano
   > piling high
   > shapes its horizon levels.

10. In blizzards, blurred small Indian cayuses
    drifted like iceburgs, furred, a dirty white.
    Browsed among wild crocuses. Stampeded
    like weathered black machines,
    their pistons shaking
    tiger lily, dog rose.

11. Unlighted fireworks—
    the bright Sarcees
    slumbered among us in a dream.
    Chiefs in their eagle-feather haloes—
    intricate beadwork, quillwork,
    (stipple, stroke).
    Upright papooses, portable in quivers,
    black-eyed as saskatoons.

12. Wind whipping us, rain pricking,
    poplars bending.
    Through a stream of all my hair,
    gleam of my father's spurs,
    our jingling bridles,
    the grave-box, lidless, open
    where we rode:

    string figure in bangles and rags.
    Small corpse picked to the bone.

            Dusk fell.
            In all my cells dusk fell.

            My shroud or winding sheet.

            O bind me
            tight against this eye
            this prairie eye
            that stares and stares.

            O hide me safe
            in cleft or coulee

            fold me
            in leaves or blowing
            grasses.

            Hold me.

            Hold me.

THE FLOWER BED

Circular—
at a guess, twelve feet across—
and filled with a forest of sunflowers.
Girasoles turned sunward, yellow-lashed
black eyes staring at the sailing Sun.
No prospect of a blink
no fall or shift,
the focus constant, eye to eye engaged
as human eye can lock with human eye
and find within its ever-widening core,
such vastnesses of space
one's whole self tumbles in.

I see it in a glass or through a port,
crystalline,
refracting, like a globe,
its edges bending, sides distorted,
shine
of a thick lens,
the peep-hole through a door in which I *saw*
a tiny man
but *see* a bed of flowers
as bright as if enamelled yellow & green,
shooting their eye-beams at their Lord the Sun,
like so much spider's silk stretched true and taut.

And my own yellow eye, black lashed, provides
triangulation. We enmesh
three worlds with our geometry.
I learn,
in timeless Time at their green leafy school,
such silks & stares
such near-invisible straight curving lines
curving like Space itself
which merge and cross at the Omega point
and double back
to make transparent, multifoliate
Flowers of the Upper Air.

FINCHES FEEDING

They fall like feathered cones from the tree above,
sumi the painted grass where the birdseed is,
skirl like a boiling pot
or a shallow within a river—
a bar of gravel breaking the water up.

Having said that, what have I said?
Not much.

Neither my delight nor the length of my watching is
                                                    conveyed
and nothing profound recorded, yet these birds
as I observe them
stir such feelings up—
such yearnings for weightlessness, for hollow bones,
rapider heartbeat, east/west eyes
and such wonder—seemingly half-remembered—as they rise
spontaneously into air, like feathered cones.

FOR ARTHUR

When earth quaked
and lintel shook
my only thought
to shout:

I love you, love you.

WATER AND MARBLE

And shall I tell him that the thought of him
turns me to water
and when his name is spoken pale still sky
trembles and breaks and moves like blowing water
that winter thaws its frozen drifts in water
all matter blurs, unsteady, seen through water
and I, in him, dislimn, water in water?

As true: the thought of him
has made me marble
and when his name is spoken blowing sky
settles and freezes in a dome of marble
and winter seals its floury drifts in marble
all matter double-locks as dense as marble
and I, in other's eyes, am cut from marble.

DOMESTIC POEM FOR A SUMMER AFTERNOON

The yellow garden-chair is newly-webbed.
There, Arthur, full-length, reads of 'Toronto the Golden',
dozes, nods, lets fall his magazine.
From a golden book I read of Arthur, the King,
and Taliessen, the King's poet. I dream of the crown.
Was it jewelled with rubies, emeralds, stones the colour of
                                        his eyes?

The ducks are within arm's reach as usual
at this time in the afternoon—two mallards, webbed
feet tucked out of sight, they float
in unreflecting emerald grass. They doze.
Might be decoys, these wild water birds
unmoving as wood.

It is hot. Siesta-still.
Not hot enough for Brazil but I think of Brazil
and the small yellow bird that flew in and perched
on the toe of Arthur's crossed-over foot,
puffed out its feathers, settled down for the night;
and the humming-bird, ruby-throated, a glowing coal
with the noise of a jet
which landed cool and light on the crown of his head.

We are settled down for the afternoon,
with whispering sprinklers and whirring jets.
We are so motionless we might be decoys
placed here by higher hunters who watch from their blind.
Arthur asleep has the face of a boy.
Like blue obsidian the drake's head glints.
His mate and I are brown in feather and skin
and above us the midsummer sun, crown of the sky,
shines indiscriminate down on duck and man.

REMEMBERING GEORGE JOHNSTON READING

A slow January, grey, the weather rainy.
Day after day after day the ceiling zero.
Then you arrive, comb honey from your hives pulled from
your suitcase, head full of metrics, syllable count,
rhyme—half-hidden, half rhyme and alliteration—
the poem's skeleton and ornamentation—
to give a reading as untheatrical as
it is subtle, elegant and unexpected.

I had not anticipated your translations
from Old Norse, your saga of heroic Gisli—
good man, strong man, man who could split an enemy
as butchers split a chicken, clean through the breastbone—
driven to running bloody, head drenched in redness,
dreamer of dark dreams prophetic of his downfall.
Writer of scaldic verses. Gisli, crow-feeder.
Great Gisli, dead of great wounds, son of whey-Thorbjorn.

Nor had I been prepared for those scaldic verse forms
(three-stressed lines in four pairs, final foot trochaic)
that made my head hum—their intricate small magic
working away like yeast till eight lines of court metre
are glittering and airy, furnished with pianos,
each short line, inexplicably a pianist
recreating for me the music of Scarlatti—
crossing hands on the keyboard, crossing and crossing.

Or—working away like bees in blossoms, shaking
a pollen of consonants on the audience
which sat, bundled and bunched in mufflers and greatcoats
in the bare unwelcoming hall where poets read
in Victoria, city of rainy winters.
And thinking about it now, I remember sun
and how honey sweetened the verses, made them gold
and tasting, that mid-January, of field-flowers.

SHORT SPRING POEM
FOR THE SHORT-SIGHTED

Arabis
clotted cream
in the rockery

Framed by shrubs'
differing greens
the daffodils:
softgolden stars on stilts

Jonquils
red-eyed as vireos
peer out

And all the trees are clouds
pink clouds   or white
anchored by rusty hawsers

clouds of green
busy and airy
as a swarm of gnats

Soon now
the squeaky tulips
will cry 'O'

and 'O'

CONCHITA KNOWS WHO WHO IS

Quien sabe, Senora? Quien sabe?
  Conchita speaks.
Who broke the plate, Conchita?
Quien sabe, Senora?
What day of the week?
Who knows?
What time of day?
Quien sabe? Quien sabe, Senora?
  Boredom. Despair. Evasion.
  Shades of unknowing.
Where is the key?
Conchita, whose shoes are these?
Quien sabe, Senora? Quien sabe.
Who knows? Who knows.

  Who knows.
  A statement of fact.
  Of faith.
  WHO knows.
  Who knows who is this WHO?
  Conchita knows.
  Conchita knows WHO knows who broke the plate,
  what day, what hour, who stands beside the gate
  and where the key, and whose the shoes . . .
  Conchita knows who WHO is,
  one vast WHO
  in whom all questions are resolved
  all answers hiding.

Quien sabe, Senora. Quien sabe.
  Indulgent. Wise.
  Don't worry *your* head about it, child.
  WHO knows.

STEFAN

Stefan
aged eleven
looked at the baby and said
When he thinks it must be pure thought
because he hasn't any words yet
and we
proud parents
admiring friends
who had looked at the baby

looked at the baby again

MOTEL POOL

The plump good-natured children play in the blue pool:
roll and plop; plop and roll;

slide and tumble, oiled, in the slippery sun
silent as otters, turning over and in,

churning the water; or—seamstresses—cut and sew
with jack-knives its satins invisibly.

Not beautiful, but suddenly limned with light
their elliptical wet flesh in a flash reflects it

and it greens the green grass, greens the hanging leaf
greens Adam and Eden, greens little Eve.

PHONE CALL FROM MEXICO

Over the years and miles   your
voice   weeping
telling me you are old
have lost your mind
and all the winds and waters of
America
sound in your words

I see your house
a square-cut topaz   set
within a larger   square
tangle of garden
walled
Brick walls
wild dahlias
raspberry canes and dogs
Raised ladies' flowerbeds
crammed with mignonettes
lobelias
little red-eyes
all the buzz
and hum of summer
It is hot
The golden sun rains down
its golden dust
upon you   shrunken
toothless   lonely   I
do not know this
person
Elinor
Don't know   can't see
you as you say you are
a shrivelled pod

rattling   rasping
a crazed creature
dazed
butting the golden air
with your goat's head
crying against
your gods your gods your gods
whom once you sensed
benign caretakers of
the realms   dominions of
your provenance
and now know baneful
black   obsidian
to be confronted
and destroyed

How tell you they
are ungods
Elinor?
How urge you to unlock
and put aside
your clumsy armour
manic armaments
and impotent blind rage?
to lay your head
down gently
like a quarrelsome
tired child?

A phone call
will not do
cannot give comfort   can
not thorns extract
nor antidote
force down
Over this distance
cannot touch your hand

Your voice is broken arrows
You are all
those whom I love
who age ungainly
whose
joints   hearts   psyches
minds   unhinge
and whom
I cannot mend
or ease

How do we end
this phone call
Elinor?
You
railing and roiling
over miles and years
And I
in tears

MASQUERADERS

What curious masks we wear:
bald patches and grey hair
who once wore dark or fair.

Wear too much flesh or none—
a scrag of skin and bone.
The gold gone.

Bi-focalled and watch-bound
who once, time out of mind
glimpsed world without end.

Worse masquerades to come:
white cane, black gaping tomb
as if we were blind, dead, lame

who, in reality, are
dark, fair and shinier
than the masks we wear or wore.

DWELLING PLACE

This habitation—bones and flesh and skin—
where I reside, proceeds through sun and rain
a mobile home with windows and a door
and pistons plunging, like a soft machine.

Conforming as a bus, its 'metal' is
more sensitive than chrome or brass. It knows
a pebble in its shoe or heat or cold.
I scrutinize it through some aperture

that gives me godsview—see it twist and change.
It sleeps, it weeps, its poor heart breaks,
it dances like a bear, it laughs, opines
(and therefore *is*). It has a leafy smell

of being young in all the halls of heaven.
It serves a term in anterooms of hell,
greying and losing lustre. It is dull.
A lifeless empty skin. I plot its course

and watch it as it moves—a house, a bus;
I, its inhabitant, indweller—eye
to that tiny chink where two worlds meet—
or—if you so discern it—two divide.

THE TETHERS

You are my tethers—you and you and you:
beautiful, ailing, witty or beloved.
You hold my tent-pole upright
make my tent
symmetrical and true—
you guy-ropes of a tent
that would not be a tent.

Think what a sail I'd make
against the blue—
flying!—for God's sake.
What a splendid din
the whip and rattle of my canvas wings
flapping me upward
ragged as a crane.

Not as I dreamed:
tent formless, beyond form.
But as I never dreamed:
tent shapeless, without shape.

A GRAVE ILLNESS

Someone was shovelling gravel all that week.
The flowering plums came out.
Rose-coloured streets
branched in my head—
spokes of a static wheel
spinning and whirring only when I coughed.
And sometimes, afterwards, I couldn't tell
if I had coughed or he had shovelled. Which.

Someone was shovelling until it hurt.
The rasp of metal on cement, the scrape
and fall
of all that broken rock.
Such industry day after day. For what?
My cough's accompanist?
The flowering trees
blossomed behind my eyes in drifts of red
delicate petals. I was hot.
The shovel grated in my breaking chest.

Someone was shovelling gravel. Was it I?
Burying me in shifts and shards of rock
up to my gasping throat. My head was out
dismembered, sunken-eyed
as John the Baptist's on a plate.
Meanwhile the plum
blossoms trickling from above
through unresistant air
fell on my eyes and hair
as crimson as my blood.

EVENING DANCE OF THE GREY FLIES

For Chris

Grey flies, fragile, slender-winged and slender-legged
scribble a pencilled script across the sunlit lawn.

As grass and leaves grow black
the grey flies gleam—
their cursive flight a gold calligraphy.

It is the light that gilds their frail
bodies, makes them fat and bright as bees—
reflected or refracted light—

as once my fist
burnished by some beam I could not see
glowed like gold mail and conjured Charlemagne

as once your face
grey with illness and with age—
a silverpoint against the pillow's white—

shone suddenly like the sun
before you died.

TO A DEAD FRIEND

I miss your letters   Fail to connect
To find
ways to connect
Can you
help? Surely
from where you are—where are you?—your view
is better than the view I have
which is
short

Can you see back and
forward yet?   Or
what I mean is
is your time vertical?
If so   how
high?
Right out of sight?
You   I
invisible   each to each?
Or you   invisible
and I
enmeshed   fleshed out
in space?

So   if you cared to
could you see   me
failing to find
ways to connect?
And could you help?
Or   what I mean is
will you?

YOUR HAND ONCE . . .

All crippled. All with flaws.
You, me
the wheeling young
buds blind on their stalk
eggs
sealed against sun . . .

Tuck it all up.
Turn it in.

Yet there where no flaw shows
in the full sunlight
that
bright spot, lancing sight
dancing dazzle of motes . . .
your hand once
your face
swam in that light
and shone.

ABOUT DEATH

And at the moment of death
what is correct procedure?

Cut the umbilicus, they said.

And with the umbilicus cut
how then prepare the body?

Wash it in sacred water.
Dress it in silk for the wedding.

AT SEA

*True devotion is for itself: not
to desire heaven nor to fear hell.*

   — RABIA EL-ADEWIA, 8th c.

Rounding the salt-rimed deck
riding the tilting sea
sky grey
seabirds wheeling,
head down in despair,
in treadmill trapped,
in thoughts
revolving, churning, churning;
a stranger from a chair,
(one I had passed before
how many times unseeing?)
rose—and as if her words
were butterfly or bird
lighting upon my wrist,
blue butterfly of Brazil,
hoopoe perhaps or rare
landbird from who-knows-where,
weightless upon my wrist,
trembling brilliant there—
stopped the machine and brought
its grinding to a halt

and in that silence spoke

I don't know what she said
only that my despair
vanished and standing there
sky grey
seabirds wheeling
I knew as I looked at her
tweed coat and blowing hair
that she was Rabia.

THE SELVES

Every other day I am an invalid.
Lie back among the pillows and white sheets
lackadaisical O lackadaisical.
Brush my hair out like a silver fan.
Allow myself to be wheeled into the sun.
Calves' foot jelly, a mid-morning glass of port,
these I accept and rare azaleas in pots.

The nurses humour me. They call me 'dear'.
I am pilled and pillowed into another sphere
and there my illness rules us like a queen,
is absolute monarch, wears a giddy crown
and I, its humble servant at all times, am its least
serf on occasion and excluded from the feast.

Every other *other* day I am as fit
as planets circling.
I brush my hair into a golden sun,
strike roses from a bush,
rare plants in pots
blossom within the green of my eyes, I am
enviable O I am enviable.

Somewhere in between the two, a third
wishes to speak, cannot make itself heard,
stands unmoving, mute, invisible,
a bolt of lightning in its naked hand.

IN CLASS WE CREATE OURSELVES—HAVING BEEN TOLD TO SHUT OUR EYES, AND GIVEN A PIECE OF PLASTICENE WITH WHICH TO MODEL A PERSON

For Judith

We made them with shut eyes—little figurines.
Worked away at them with our fingers, our whole bodies
straining to create them—foreheads, mouths,
even our leg muscles tensed in their making.

When I opened my eyes, the so-obvious form I'd worked on
was not what I had thought. A naked woman
the size of my hand. Flesh-pink. Blind.
I couldn't tell if she was cradling an invisible child.

The man beside me said that she was sleeping.
Possibly self-protective. I thought that his
was crucified or crying, 'Help me!'—spare,
male, square, as if cut with a tool.

No two of them siblings. One like a bowl—
lap, a receptacle, torso a kind of handle;
one covered all over with small, irregular lumps;
one on her side, abstracted, refusing an offering.

Who made them? I wondered. Surely not we who observed them.
Somebody deeper, detached, had a hand in this making—
moulded the plasticene, followed the blue-print.
And who was it we fashioned? Which self was the self we created?—

so like, yet so unlike—a nearly identical twin
in miniature, not fully gestated,
which struggled out of us through our ignorant fingers
bearing its curious message—*noli me tangere*.

SUFFERING

*"Man is made in such a way that he is never so much
attached to anything as he is to his suffering."* —GURDJIEFF

Suffering
confers identity. It makes you proud.
The one bird in the family bush. Which other, ever
suffered so? Whose nights, whose days,
a thicket of blades to pass through?
Deeps of tears. Not ever to give it up
this friend whose sword
turns in your heart,
this o-so-constant clever cove—care-giver
never neglectful, saying yes and yes
to plumed funerary horses, to grey drizzle
falling against the panes of the eyes.

Oh, what without it . . . ? If you turned your back?
Unthinkable, so to reject it, choose instead
meadows flower-starred
or taste, for instance—just for an instant—bread.
The sweet-smelling fields of the earth
dancing
goldenly dancing
in your mouth.

But
suffering is sweeter yet.
That dark embrace—that birthmark,
birthright, even.
Yours forever
ready to be conjured up—
tongue in the sore tooth, fingertip
pressed to the bandaged cut
and mind returning to it over and over.

Best friend, bestower of feeling
status-giver.
Something to suck at like a stone.
One's own. One's owner.
. . . One's almost lover.

DEEP SLEEP

Moon and sun of no account.
The silver days—sky full of pearls at midday
and the lake of polished platinum—these
she has not even noticed.
Neither the two hawks circling nor the snake
coiled and blinking
by the path to the dock.
For she is in deep sleep.
She dreams and then forgets
the little plays she dreams,
small one-act personal versions of
Troilus and Cressida, of Psyche's lamp
which burns the sleeping Eros with its oil.

Where is the slow unpeopled beach she lies on?
What the leaves' talk, waves' lisp,
'o-sweet-canada-canada' shrill from a bush?
No noisy outboard breaks the spell
that wraps her round and round in silken threads—
a spindle for the spun stuff of midsummer—
as skein on skein it mutes her senses, dulls
the bright enamelled world in which she walks.

I wait to see her wake. Shed sleep like bedding.
Slip naked into day, coloured and quick.
Register sunlit pines, the tiny pound
of rain on canvas, knife-blade light on water—
but cannot wait forever, cannot wait
forever. Cannot
wait.

THE NEW BICYCLE

All the molecules in the house
re-adjust on its arrival,
make way for its shining presence
its bright dials,
and after it has settled
and the light
has explored its surfaces
—and the night—
they compose themselves again
in another order.

One senses the change at once
without knowing what one senses.
Has somebody cleaned the windows
used different soap
or is there a bowl of flowers
on the mantelpiece?—
for the air makes another shape
it is thinner or denser,
a new design
is invisibly stamped upon it.

How we all adapt ourselves
to the bicycle
aglow in the furnace room,
turquoise where turquoise
has never before been seen,
its chrome gleaming
on gears and pedals,
its spokes glistening.
Lightly resting on the incised
rubber of its airy tires
it has changed us all.

INTRAOCULAR LENS MODEL 103G

This lens I look through is as clear as glass.
It shows me all I saw before was false.

If what *was* true is true no longer, how
now can I know the false true from true true?

CONCENTRATION

Shall I break the bones of my head
in a nutcracker?
Brain-break. Mind-break.

The room in a trice turns black.

The fontanelles open
a fraction of a second

something shimmering whizzes out.

VISITANTS

Each afternoon at four bird after bird
soars in and lands in the branches of the oaks.
They stamp about like policemen. Thick boots
almost visible in the lacy leaves.
No, those are birds, not boots, clumsy, heavy
leaf-rustlers who tear at twigs and rend
the living bone of the tortured trees and pelt
the lawn below—thup,thup,thup—with acorns.
They give no cry, no coo—a flock of mutes
overhead, deaf-mutes perhaps, unhearing
the flail and storm they make stuffing, stuffing
their gullets and sleek bellies with salad fruits.

Through binoculars they are beautiful,
the prettiest pigeons—every feather
each neat little head, white collar, banded tail.
But voracious, gang-despoilers of the tree-tops
they shake and thrash about in, tiny eyes
riveted upon acorns ah they are gone in a whoosh
wooden rackety twirling noisemakers
and we left hungry in this wingless hush.

INVISIBLE PRESENCES FILL THE AIR

I hear the clap of their folding wings
like doors banging or wooden shutters.
They land and settle—giant birds
on the epaulettes of snowed-on statues.

On grass one drops its greenest feather.
On the head of a blond boy, a yellow.
The red feather on my heart falls plumb.
Do not ask about the whitest feather.

I feel them breathing on my cheek.
They are great horses dreaming of flight.
They crowd against me. Are outsize.
Smell of sweet grass. Smell of hay.

When in my heart their hooves strike flint
a fire rages through my blood.
I want water. I want wool.
I want the fruits of citrus trees.

Their eyes flash me such mysteries
that I am famished, am ill-clad.
Dressed in the rags of my party clothes
I gather their hairs for a little suit.

O who can name me their secret names?
Anael, opener of gates.
Phorlakh, Nisroc, Heiglot,
Zlar.

DEAF-MUTE IN THE PEAR TREE

His clumsy body is a golden fruit
pendulous in the pear tree

Blunt fingers among the multitudinous buds

Adriatic blue the sky above and through
the forking twigs

Sun ruddying tree's trunk, his trunk
his massive head thick-nobbed with burnished curls
tight-clenched in bud

(Painting by Generalić. Primitive.)

I watch him prune with silent secateurs

Boots in the crotch of branches shift their weight
heavily as oxen in a stall

Hear small inarticulate mews from his locked mouth
a kitten in a box

Pear clippings fall
                    soundlessly on the ground
Spring finches sing
                    soundlessly in the leaves

A stone. A stone in ears and on his tongue

Through palm and fingertip he knows the tree's
quick springtime pulse

Smells in its sap the sweet incipient pears

Pale sunlight's choppy water glistens on
his mutely snipping blades

and flags and scraps of blue
above him make regatta of the day

But when he sees his wife's foreshortened shape
sudden and silent in the grass below
uptilt its face to him

then air is kisses, kisses

stone dissolves

his locked throat finds a little door

and through it feathered joy
flies screaming like a jay

The Dome of Heaven

TRAVELLER, CONJUROR, JOURNEYMAN

Connections and correspondences between writing and painting . . .

The idea diminishes to a dimensionless point in my absolute centre. If I can hold it steady long enough, the feeling which is associated with that point grows and fills a larger area as perfume permeates a room. It is from here that I write—held within that luminous circle, that locus which is at the same time a focusing glass, the surface of a drum.

As long as the tension (at/tention?) is sustained the work continues . . . more or less acute.

What is art anyway? What am I trying to do?

Play, perhaps. Not as opposed to work. But spontaneous involvement which is its own reward; done for the sheer joy of doing it; for the discovery, invention, sensuous pleasure. 'Taking a line for a walk', manipulating sounds, rhythms.

Or transposition. At times I seem to be attempting to copy exactly something which exists in a dimension where worldly senses are inadequate. As if a thing only felt had to be extracted from invisibility and transposed into a seen thing, a heard thing. The struggle is to fit the 'made' to the 'sensed' in such a way that the whole can occupy a world larger than the one I normally inhabit. This process involves scale. Poem or painting is by-product.

Remembering, re-membering, re-capturing, re-calling, re-collecting . . . words which lead to the very threshold of some thing, some place; veiled by a membrane at times translucent, never yet transparent, through which I long to be absorbed.

Is it I who am forgotten, dismembered, escaped, deaf, uncollected?

Already I have lost yesterday and the day before. My childhood is a series of isolated vignettes, vivid as hypnagogic visions. Great winds have blown my past away in gusts leaving patches and parts of my history and pre-history. No wonder I want to remember, to follow a thread back. To search for something I already know but have forgotten I know. To listen—not to but for.

I am a two-dimensional being. I live in a sheet of paper. My home has length and breadth and very little thickness. The tines of a fork pushed vertically through the paper appear as four thin silver ellipses. I may, in a moment of insight, realize that it is more than coincidence that four identical but independent silver rings have entered my world. In a further breakthrough I may glimpse their unity, even sense the entire fork—large, glimmering, extraordinary. Just beyond my sight. Mystifying; marvellous.

My two-dimensional consciousness yearns to catch some overtone which will convey that great resonant silver object.

Expressed another way—I am traveller. I have a destination but no maps. Others perhaps have reached that destination already, still others are on their way. But none has had to go from here before—nor will again. One's route is one's own. One's journey unique. What I will find at the end I can barely guess. What lies on the way is unknown.

How to go? Land, sea or air? What techniques to use? What vehicle?

I truly think I do not write or draw for you or you or you . . . whatever you may argue to the contrary. Attention excludes you. You do not exist. I am conscious only of being 'hot' or 'cold' in relation to some unseen centre.

Without magic the world is not to be borne. I slightly misquote from Hesse's *Conjectural Biography*. A prisoner, locked in his cell, he paints all the things that have given him pleasure in life—trees, mountains, clouds. In the middle of his canvas he places a small train, its engine already lost in a tunnel. As the prison guards approach to lead Hesse off to still further deprivations, he makes himself small and steps aboard his little train which continues on its way and vanishes. For a while its sooty smoke drifts from the tunnel's mouth, then it slowly blows away and 'with it the whole picture and I with the picture'.

Magic, that Great Divide, where everything reverses. Where all laws change. A good writer or painter understands these laws and practises conjuration.

Yes, I would like to be a magician.

One longs for an art that would satisfy all the senses—not as in

184

opera or ballet where the separate arts congregate—but a complex intermingling—a consummate More-Than. This is perhaps just another way of saying one longs for the senses themselves to merge in one supra-sense.

Not that there aren't marriages enough between the arts—some inevitably more complete than others. But no ménage à trois. Let alone four or five.

Trying to see these categories and their overlaps in terms of writing and painting I start a rough chart:

WRITING		WRITING/PAINTING	PAINTING	
Aural	*Visual*	*Marriage*	*Calligraphic*	*Painterly*
Poetry written to be spoken: Chambers' *Fire*.	Some of Herbert's poems	Arabesques	Klee	Monet
		Concrete poetry	Tobey	etc.
	Dylan Thomas' *Vision and Prayer*	bill bissett's 'typewriter poems' etc.	etc.	
Poetry written to be sung: Cohen's *Suzanne* etc.	e. e. cummings etc.	Illuminated Ms.		

I get only so far when I stop. Too many ideas rush at me. The categories shift and merge in such a way that I am at times unable to distinguish even between the visual and the aural. John Chambers' recording of his poem *Fire* brings me up short. This is an aural poem. It relies for its effect on long silences between words—the silences as significant as the words themselves. If one wants to reproduce this poem on paper one can use the conventions of musical transcription *or* one can so space the words on the page that the poem becomes . . . visual. What is time to the ear becomes space to the eye.

'In not being two everything is the same.'

Moving through the category 'Marriage' to 'Calligraphic' and 'Painterly' one must come at length to pure colour. No form at all. And moving from 'Marriage' through 'Visual' and 'Aural' one must finally arrive at pure sound—no words at all.

The notes of the scale: the colours of the rainbow.

'A Father said to his double-seeing son: "Son, you see two instead of one." "How can that be?" the boy replied. "If I were, there would seem to be *four* moons up there in place of two".' (Hakim Sanai of Ghazna.)

If writing and painting correspond at the primary level as I believe they do, how and where do they differ?

With a poem I am given a phrase. Often when I least expect it. When my *mind* is on something else. And my hands busy. Yet it must be caught at once, for it comes like a boomerang riding a magical arc and, continuing its forward path, it will vanish unless intercepted. And that phrase contains the poem as a seed contains the plant.

It is also the bridge to another world where the components of the poem lie hidden like the parts of a dismembered statue in an archaeological site. They need to be sought and found and painstakingly put together again. And it is the search that matters. When the final piece slips into place the finished poem seems no more important than the image in a completed jig-saw puzzle. Worth little more than a passing glance.

Painting or drawing the process is entirely different. I start from no where. I am given no thing. The picture, born at pen-point, grows out of the sensuous pleasure of nib, lead or brush moving across a surface. It has its own senses this activity: varieties of tactile experience, rhythms. Beating little drums, strumming taut strings. And sometimes there is the curious impression of a guiding hand— as if I am hanging on to the opposite end of some giant pen which is moving masterfully and hugely in some absolute elsewhere, and my small drawing—lesser in every way—is nevertheless related, a crabbed inaccurate approximation.

Yet in all essential particulars writing and painting are interchangeable. They are alternate roads to silence.

1970

QUESTIONS AND IMAGES

The last ten years span three distinct places—and phases—in my life: Brazil, Mexico, Canada, in that order. All countries of the new world.

Brazil pelted me with images. Marmosets in the flowering jungle; bands of multi-coloured birds moving among the branches of the kapok tree outside the bedroom verandah; orchids in the kapok tree, cucumbers in the kapok tree, the whole tree bursting into cotton candy. Flamboyantes in flaming flower against the sky as one lay on one's back in the swimming pool. Doric palms waving green plumage, growing antlers and beads. Cerise dragon flies. Butterflies as large as a flying hand and blue, bright blue.

Drums from the favelas beat like one's own blood, accompanied by the deep bass viol of frogs in the lotus pond; volleys of rockets shattered the black night air, air wet as a sheet and rank with the smell of decaying jackos. Insistent, less obtrusive, the tiny fret of tropical vegetation, the sibilance of bamboos.

Churches, golden as the eye of God, were so miraculously proportioned that one wondered if proportion alone might actually alter consciousness. Enormous quantities of gold leaf. Entire interiors of it, changing space, vibrating strangely; at one moment flashing to blind you, at another reverberating on and on like a golden gong. Moorish designs in tiles and lattices created infinities of intricate repetition.

My first foreign language—to live in, that is—and the personality changes that accompany it. One is a toy at first, a doll. Then a child. Gradually, as vocabulary increases, an adult again. But a different adult. Who am I, then, that language can so change me? What is personality, identity? And the deeper change, the profounder understanding—partial, at least—of what man is, devoid of words. Where could wordlessness lead? Shocks, insights, astounding and sudden walls. Equally astounding and sudden dematerializations; points of view shifting and vanishing. Attitudes recognized for what they are: attitudes. The Word behind the word . . . but when there *is* no word . . . ?

('Why did you stop writing?' 'I didn't. It stopped.' 'Nonsense, you're the master.' 'Am I?') Who would not, after all, be a poet, a good poet, if one could choose? If one could choose. Most of one's life one has the illusion of choice. And when that is removed, when clearly one cannot choose. . . . Blank page after blank page. The thing I had feared most of all had happened at last. This time I never *would* write again. But by some combination of factors—coincidence, serendipity—the pen that had written was now, most surprisingly, drawing. ('Why did you start drawing?' 'I didn't. It started.' 'But why start something you know nothing about and chuck up all the techniques and skills. . . ?') Why, indeed, why?

What was that tiny fret, that wordless dizzying vibration, the whole molecular dance? Is that what Tobey's white writing wrote? What was that golden shimmer, the bright pink shine on the anturias, the delicately and exactly drawn design of the macaw's feathers? Why did I suddenly see with the eye of an ant? Or a fly? The golden—yes, there it was again—web spun by the spider among the leaves of the century plant? Surely the very purpose of a web demands invisibility? Yet this was a lure, a glistening small sun, jewelled already with opalescent victims. Victims of what?

The impotence of a marmoset in a rage, pitting itself against me, its fingers like the stems of violets, unable to break the skin of my hand. How quickly one learns about scale with a marmoset for companion. Man in a rage with his gods, or, equally superficially, pleased with them. The glorious macaw, the flesh of his Groucho Marx face wrinkled and soft, his crazy hilarious laughter and low seductive chuckles making him kin until one looked into his infinitely dilatable eye and was drawn through its vortex into a minute cosmos which contained all the staggering dimensions of outer space.

I wonder now if 'brazil' would have happened wherever I was? As to where it pointed I hadn't the least idea, nor, I think, did I ask any questions beyond the immediate ones. But I drew as if my life depended on it—each tile of each house, each leaf of each tree, each blade of grass, each mote of sunlight—all things bright and beautiful. If I drew them all. . . ? And I did. Compelled, propelled by the point of my pen. And in drawing them all I seemed to make them mine, or make peace with them, or they with me. And then, having drawn everything—each drop of water and grain of sand—the pen began dreaming. It began a life of its own.

Looking back with my purely psychological eye through the long clear topaz of that day, I appear as a mute observer, an inarticulate listener, occupying another part of myself.

If Brazil was day, then Mexico was night. All the images of darkness hovered for me in the Mexican sunlight. If Brazil was a change of place, then Mexico was a change of time. One was very close to the old gods here. Death and the old gods. Their great temples rose all around one. Temples to the Sun. Temples to the Moon.

Objects dissolved into their symbols. All the pyramids and stairs, plumed serpents in stone, masks of jade, obsidian knives, skulls of crystal—or sugar.

In the rain forest stood the bone-white ruins of buildings—tangible remains of a whole mythology. Buildings so intricate—(tarsal, metatarsal)—one was tempted to believe they were skeletons from which the flesh had long since rotted. Motionless. Beautiful. Great ivory kings and queens beneath their lacy cranial combs. Palaces and gardens of the Sleeping Beauty.

The villages seemed unchanged since the beginning of time. The same adobe huts, the same fields of maize, the same ancient languages of clicking consonants, and surely, the same gods. Gods hungry for human blood. (Too much Lowry and Lawrence?) The plazas of Catholic churches were stages for the old rituals of costumed dances, stamped out to the music of conch shell and drum.

In Oaxaca the women of Yalalag wear triple crosses which led Cortés's priests to the mistaken belief that Christian missionaries had preceded them. Oaxacans perhaps understand the symbolism of the cross: time passing, time eternal—'the intersection of this world with eternity'. In Chichen Itza the Caracol or Snail—an observatory dome from which the Mayans probed the heavens—has four small openings exactly pointing to the cardinal directions. Temples of the Cross. Temples of the Foliated Cross.

Coming as I do from a random or whim-oriented culture, this recurrence and interrelating of symbols into an ordered and significant pattern—prevalent too in the folk arts of pottery and weaving —was curiously illuminating. One did not feel restricted by the enclosed form of the 'design'; rather, one was liberated into something life-giving and larger. I could now begin to understand how the 'little world is created according to the prototype of the great world'.

Great or little, for me it was still a night world—one into which the pattern was pricked like a constellation—bright, twinkling, hard to grasp, harder still to hold. A dreaming world in which I continued to draw and to dream. How to make a noumenal doll; how to fly; the man with one black and one white hand—(Hari-Hara?); Osiris— (The Seat of the Eye); the room with the invisible walls; the circular dance beside the sea—(Initiation? Into what? A non-religious Christian? A religious non-Christian?) Poetry was more than ever now in the perceiving. My only access to it was through the dream and the drawing.

I had my first two shows during this period. The age of my graphic innocence was past. I had acquired another mask, another label.

Each additional one seemed to move me further from my own centre. I was now suddenly and sharply reminded of the young Rilke, bored on a rainy afternoon, coming upon the clothing and paraphernalia of disguise in the wardrobes of a spare room; and how, masked, turbanned and cloaked, he had struck a pose before a mirror. 'I stared', he wrote, 'at this great, terrifying unknown personage before me and it seemed appalling to me that I should be alone with him.'

Which is the mask and which the self? How distinguish, let alone separate, two such seemingly interpenetrating matters? As if pursued by the Hound of Heaven I raced back and forth among the *Collected Works* of Jung, *The Perennial Philosophy*, *The Doors of Perception*, Zen, C. S. Lewis, St John of the Cross.

'See how he who thinks himself one is not one, but seems to have as many personalities as he has moods.'

'Understand that thou thyself art even another little world, and hast within thee the sun and the moon, and also the stars . . .'

I began to suspect, in what would once have been near-heresy, that drawing and writing were not only ends in themselves, as I had previously thought, but possibly the means to an end which I could barely imagine—a method, perhaps, of tracing the 'small design'. And the very emergence of these ideas began to clear a way, remove the furniture and provide a new space.

But when something one has thought opaque appears translucent, transparent even, one questions whether it might not ultimately become entirely invisible. Solid walls dissolved disconcertingly into scrims. For the moment I was uncertain where to lean.

The dark Mexican night had led me back into myself and I was startlingly aware of the six directions of space.

A day and a night had passed. My return to Canada, if the pattern continued, should be the start of a new day.

The culture shock of homecoming after many years abroad is even greater, I think, than the culture shock of entering a new country. One returns different, to a different place, misled by the belief that neither has changed. Yet I am grateful for the shocks. The conditioning process which turns live tissue into fossil is arrested by the earthquake. Even buried strata may be exposed.

I had a small retrospective show shortly after coming home, followed by the publication of a book of 'retrospective' poetry. The shutting of twin doors. Not necessarily on drawings and poems but on *those* drawings and *those* poems.

The questions had now become more pressing than the images. Some of the questions were retrospective: had the move from writing to drawing been a return to the primitive in myself—to the 'first man' of Van der Post? Was it a psychological starting again from

190

the pre-verbal state? If in the life of the individual and the life of the race, drawing precedes written literature, was this step back really a beginning? Certainly the varied scenes through which I had journeyed had provided no lack of subject matter.

More urgent, however, were the questions raised by Alan McGlashan: 'Who or what is the Dreamer within us? To whom is the Dreamer talking?' What, indeed, is this duologue, so like an effortless poem? Can projected images be manifested as dreams? Are all dreams projected? Or some? Is the Dreamer active or passive? Initiator or recipient? Sometimes one, sometimes the other? And what about the waking Dreamer? Are thoughts the invisible dreams of a daylight world? Projected by what, or whom? Jung's collective unconscious? Rumi's angels?

I don't know the answers to these questions but merely posing them moves more furniture. I begin to sense another realm—inter-related—the high doh of a scale in which we are the low. And in a sudden and momentary bouleversement, I realize that I have been upside down in life—like a tree on its head, roots exposed in the air.

The question of the mask which confronted me with such violence in Mexico has subtly shifted. In our popcorn packages when I was a child, along with the tin rings, jacks, marbles and other hidden surprises, one was occasionally lucky enough to find a small coloured picture complete with strips of transparent red and green celluloid. The picture, viewed alone, was of a boy with an umbrella and a dog. Seen through the green filter, the umbrella disappeared. The red filter demolished the dog. My subconscious evidently knew something about the tyranny of subjectivity years ago when it desired to go 'through to the area behind the eyes/where silent, unrefractive white-ness lies'. I didn't understand the image then but it arrived complete. It was not to be denied even though only half-glimpsed, enigmatic. It's pleasant now to know what I was talking about!

Whether or not the handful of poems written recently means that writing has 'started' again, I do not know; whether there is any advance over earlier work, I shall have to let others decide. For the time being my primary concern is to remove the filters.

Meanwhile the images have begun again and the questions continue. 'What do I sing and what does my lute sing?'

1969